C000179353

LIVING STONES

PEBBLES

SUSAN SAYERS

Illustrated by
Arthur Baker

Kevin Mayhew

First published in 1999 by
KEVIN MAYHEW LTD
Buxhall
Stowmarket
Suffolk IP14 3BW

© 1999 Susan Sayers

The right of Susan Sayers to be identified as the author
of this work has been asserted by her in accordance
with the Copyright, Designs and Patents Act 1988.

All rights reserved. No part of this publication may be reproduced,
stored in a retrieval system, or transmitted, in any form or by any means,
electronic, mechanical, photocopying, recording or otherwise,
without the prior written permission of the publisher.

The contents of this book may be photocopied without copyright infringement, provided
they are used for the purpose for which they are intended. Reproduction of any of the contents
of this book for commercial purposes is subject to the usual copyright restrictions

0 1 2 3 4 5 6 7 8 9

ISBN 1 84003 397 5
Catalogue No. 1500291

The other titles in the *Living Stones* series are

Complete Resource Book	ISBN 1 84003 396 7	Cat. No. 1500290
Prayers of Intercession	ISBN 1 84003 395 9	Cat. No. 1500294
Rocks	ISBN 1 84003 398 3	Cat. No. 1500292
Boulders	ISBN 1 84003 399 1	Cat. No. 1500293

Cover photographs:
Two small children – courtesy of SuperStock Ltd, London
Background – courtesy of Images Colour Library Ltd, London
Cover design by Jaquetta Sergeant
Edited by Katherine Laidler
Typesetting by Jonathan Stroulger
Printed in Great Britain

FOREWORD

For this age group the world is opening out from the immediate family circle, and full of possibilities. The children are becoming aware of familiar faces Sunday by Sunday, and now they are brought in to join the big children for Sunday school. It can be a daunting prospect, and the way young children are met and welcomed, talked and listened to, when they first encounter the children's ministry in your church, will have a profound effect on their spiritual growth. It is through the good humour, care and friendliness of those they meet that they will begin to realise how God loves them.

In all your planning, keep aware of how it will seem from the children's point of view. Is the area attractive and inviting? Does the furniture fit? Is the atmosphere orderly and therefore unthreatening? Are people talking at a speed they can cope with, and giving them time to reply without pressure? Do people genuinely seem to like them and want them to be happy? Is considerate love and fairness expressed in actions as well as in the teaching? Is it a place where they can relax and feel at home? Is it fun?

These things are so important because the children will be learning far more from the way things are done and from the people they work with, than from the actual teaching content, valuable as this obviously is. It is a good idea to review your aims and objectives annually, setting out for yourselves, the PCC, the parents, and any helpers, what you are doing and why, what works well and what needs to be tried differently. If this regular review is built into the system there is no danger of outdated methods carrying on past their sell-by date just because things have always been done like that. A termly or annual training day is also helpful in refreshing leaders and preventing cases of burn-out.

This book provides you with ideas and materials for activities for young children, all based on the CWL weekly readings. The activity sheets often include something to think and talk about together, and you can select and adapt the ideas to suit your particular group. Vary the media the children work with – crayons, finger paints, sponge painting, printing, paper and fabric collage, chalks and pastels are all fun to use. Pray for the children and their families, and read the Bible passages before you plan, so as to incorporate your own valuable insights, and use the suggested games either as they stand or as starting points to help you think of other ideas of your own.

A few general ideas about story-telling:

- Tell the story from the viewpoint of a character in the situation. To create the time-machine effect, avoid eye contact as you slowly put on the appropriate cloth or cloak, and then make eye contact as you greet the children in character.

- Have an object with you which leads into the story – a water jug, or a lunch box, for instance.

- Walk the whole group through the story, so that they are physically moving from one place to another; and use all kinds of places, such as broom cupboards, under the stairs, outside under the trees, and so on.

• Collect some carpet tiles – blue and green – so that at story time the children can sit round the edge of this and help you place on the cut-outs for the story.

If parents are going to be staying with their children, involve them in the activities, or think over the possibility of having an adult discussion group in the same room, using the study material and discussion questions in the *Living Stones* Complete Resource Book. Parents are encouraged to pray with their children during the week, using the worksheet prayers.

All the material in the book is copyright-free for non-commercial use in churches and schools.

SUSAN SAYERS

CONTENTS

ORDINARY TIME

This book is dedicated to my family and friends,
whose encouraging support has been wonderful,
and to all those whose good ideas are included here for others to share.

RECOMMENDED BIBLES

It is often a good idea to look at a passage in several different versions before deciding which to use for a particular occasion.

As far as children are concerned, separate Bible stories, such as those published by Palm Tree Press and Lion, are a good introduction for the very young. Once children are reading, a very helpful version is the *International Children's Bible* (New Century version) published by Word Publishing. Here children have a translation based on experienced scholarship, using language structure suitable for young readers, with short sentences and appropriate vocabulary. There is a helpful dictionary, and clear maps and pictures are provided.

ADVENT

First Sunday of Advent

Thought for the day

Be alert and watchful; keep yourselves ready.

Readings

Isaiah 64:1-9;
Psalm 80:1-7, 17-19
1 Corinthians 1:3-9
Mark 13:24-37

Aim

To think about getting ready for Jesus.

Starter

Have three different types of music available, such as a drum, some bells, and a children's praise tape. Whenever they hear the drum they stomp about, whenever they hear the bells they run about silently on tiptoes, and whenever they hear the praise tape they dance. They will need to be ready and alert.

Teaching

Explain that today we are starting Advent which is 'getting ready' time because it means 'coming'. What's coming? Christmas! Who came to us as a baby at Christmas? Jesus!

Tell the children this rescue story.

Jake was a fisherman. When the tide came in he set off from the slipway and started the engine on his boat. Then he chugged out between the green and red buoys which showed him where the deep water was, until he reached the open sea. And there he fished and ate his sandwiches and drank his hot tea from a flask and fished some more. Jake enjoyed fishing. So did his dog, Sprat.

One day, when Jake was just halfway down his mug of hot tea, the sky got darker and darker and the wind blew stronger and stronger. The boat rocked up and down, up and down, this way and that way, and the hot tea slopped over the side of the mug, even though Jake had drunk it halfway down. Sprat made growling noises at the wind, but the wind wasn't frightened. It blew even harder.

'Dear me,' said Jake. 'This isn't a good time to be sitting out here fishing. We'd better make for home.'

He tried to start the engine but the engine just went splutter, splutter, clunk. Sprat barked at it with one ear up, to encourage it, but the engine could only go splutter, splutter, clunk.

'This is serious, Sprat,' said Jake. 'We can't stay here and we can't go home. What we need is someone to come and rescue us.'

They waited. Jake ate his other sandwich (it was tuna and salad) and Sprat had a dog biscuit, noisily. The boat went up and down, and the wind blew and blew.

Suddenly Sprat pricked up both ears and his nose twitched. He could hear something which made his tail wag. That made Jake look up. A smile began to spread over his face and he stood up, waving both arms.

'It's Bert! Hello, Bert! Ahoy there, Bert!' yelled Jake across the wind and waves.

Bert was a fisherman too, and here he was chugging over in his boat towards Jake and Sprat. 'Bert to the rescue,' he grinned.

It wasn't long before Jake had thrown a rope across from his boat to Bert's and Bert had made it fast. Jake hauled up the anchor and there they were, being towed home by Bert. It felt so good to be rescued!

When they got back to the slipway Sprat gave Bert one of his half-chewed biscuits to say thank you, and Jake treated Bert to a drink at the pub.

'We couldn't have made it home on our own, you know,' said Jake into his pint of bitter.

Bert nodded. 'Good job I came to the rescue then,' he said.

Sprat thumped his tail on the pub carpet, happy to be a rescued dog.

Talk with the children about Jake and Sprat waiting to be rescued. Long before Jesus came, the people knew they were in a mess and needed God to come to the rescue. For years and years they waited and hoped for rescue, and then Jesus came into the world. Jesus was the rescuer!

Praying

Thank you, Jesus, Son of God,
you have come to save us all.
Thank you, Jesus, Son of God,
you came because you love us all.
Amen.

Activities

During Advent the children will be making a Christmas landscape, adding to it week by week, so that it is ready to take home in time for Christmas.

The Activity Sheet for the Fourth Sunday of Advent shows what this might look like when finished.

This week the children are forming the base from crumpled paper on a shoe box lid which is covered with green paper (or painted green). There are instructions on the worksheet, together with pictures of situations in which they can be the rescuer, drawing in the badly needed help.

SECOND SUNDAY OF ADVENT

Thought for the day

John the Baptist prepares the way for the coming of the Messiah by helping the people to realign their lives.

Readings

Isaiah 40:1-11
Psalm 85:1-2, 8-13
2 Peter 3:8-15a
Mark 1:1-8

Aim

To continue getting ready for Jesus at the Christmas festival.

Starter

Involve the children in preparing a road for the game. Give each of them a longish piece of string, and help them add their piece to make a continuous winding road on the floor. Now give them a second piece of string to mark out the other side of the road in the same way. When the road is ready, choose different children to walk, hop or skip along the road.

Teaching

Point out how we all had to get the road ready before we could use it for walking, hopping and skipping along. Some of them might have seen a road being made or mended, and you can talk with them about how this has to be done very carefully so that everyone can drive and cycle on it safely.

Getting ourselves ready for Jesus is a bit like building a good road. If there are bumpy, rocky places of grumpiness and bad temper, we can start clearing them away. If there are holes in our road where we are unkind, or unfair to other people, we can fill those places up with God's love. (If you draw all this on a blackboard, then you can rub out and re-draw as you speak.)

In Advent, when we are opening the windows in our Advent calendars every day, we can get our own roads sorted out so that Jesus can walk straight into our lives without falling down holes made of our unkindness, or tripping over rocks made of our grumpiness and bad temper.

Put all kinds of boxes and 'holes' on their string road and let everyone help to clear it again. As they are clearing, comment on what they are doing: for example, 'Here's a great lump of selfishness – let's get rid of that; oh, and here's a few clumps of wanting our own way all the time – let's clear those away, too, so the road is better to walk along. That's much better, now; well done!'

Praying

Dear Jesus,
I am learning how to be kind and helpful,
I am building a good strong road of love.
Help me to build my good strong road
of kindness, goodness and truth.
Amen.

Activities

Today we are making the next stage of our Christmas landscape. We are adding the town of Bethlehem, and the road. Instructions are on the sheet, together with a picture of road building to colour.

Notes

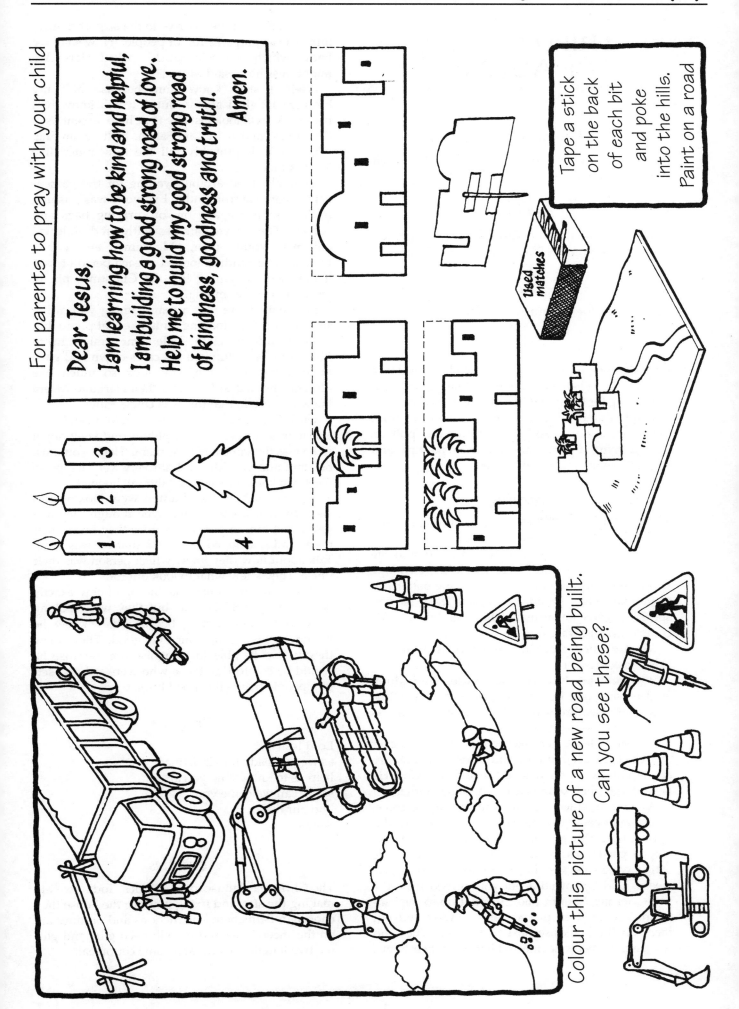

For parents to pray with your child

Dear Jesus,
I am learning how to be kind and helpful,
I am building a good strong road of love.
Help me to build my good strong road
of kindness, goodness and truth.
Amen.

Tape a stick on the back of each bit and poke into the hills. Paint on a road

Used matches

Colour this picture of a new road being built. Can you see these?

THIRD SUNDAY
OF ADVENT

Thought for the day

In Jesus, God will be fulfilling the Messianic prophecies about the promised Saviour.

Readings

Isaiah 61:1-4, 8-11; Psalm 126 or Canticle: Magnificat
1 Thessalonians 5:16-24; John 1:6-8, 19-28

Aim

To get ready for Christmas, and for Jesus.

Starter

Play some taped music which the children dance around to. Whenever the music stops, call out something for them to mime getting ready for, such as eating dinner (wash hands), driving a car (turn the ignition key), climbing a mountain (pull on boots), being a film star (put on make-up), and having a swim (changing clothes).

Teaching

Tell the children this story about waiting for someone and recognising them when they arrive.

One day the postman delivered a letter to the house where Hari and Meera lived. The envelope was pale blue, and it had a red and blue pattern all round the edge. (Hold an airmail letter as you speak.) 'That's an airmail letter,' said Hari. 'It's come from far away.'

Mum opened the letter, and read it. 'Who's it from?' asked Meera.

'It's from my brother, your uncle,' said Mum, 'and he says that he's coming to visit us. He'll be flying into Heathrow airport next month.' She was smiling and very excited.

Hari and Meera were excited too. They had never met Uncle Satich, but they had heard lots of stories about him. He sounded good fun and very kind. He never forgot their birthdays or Christmas, either.

A month seemed ages to wait for him to come. Meera kept counting the days left on the calendar until Uncle Satich was due to arrive. They all helped get Hari's room changed round, as Uncle Satich would be sleeping there as well for a few weeks. Dad borrowed a put-you-up bed from the next-door neighbours, and carried it up to the bedroom. The children picked some flowers and put them on the bookcase next to the bed. They did want him to feel welcome and happy in their home.

At last it was time to drive to the airport to meet him. The airport was full of people. 'How shall we know which is Uncle Satich?' asked Hari. 'We might miss him,' said Meera.

'Well, I shall know him, because he's my brother!' laughed Mum. 'But you will know him because he will look just like the photo he sent us at Christmas, and if I know Satich, he'll be smiling. Oh, and he'll probably tell me how much like Mother I look!'

They all stood around waiting for the passengers to come in from India. Everyone was pushing trolleys with luggage on, or carrying bags and parcels. There were families with tired children, old men, young men, old women and young women. The children looked at each person to see if they were anything like the Christmas photo, and if they were smiling.

Suddenly, there was a man coming with a big smile on his face, looking quite like that photo, but wearing different clothes. He came straight up to Mum and Dad, dumped his cases down and gave them a big hug. 'Oh, you look so much like Mother!' he said to Mum. So then Hari and Meera knew for certain that this was Uncle Satich.

Uncle Satich had stopped hugging Mum and Dad, and now he turned to the children, and knelt down so he was the same height as them. 'Hello, you must be Hari, and you Meera! I am very, very happy to meet you both!' he said. And they all hugged.

Talk about how the children were looking forward to their uncle coming even though they had never met him in person, because they knew their mum and dad loved him, and that he was kind. Talk about how they knew which person was their uncle. They knew what to look out for.

Before the first Christmas no one knew exactly what Jesus would be like, but they were looking forward to him coming because they knew he would be loving and fair and good. They knew they would be able to recognise him because he would be comforting those who were sad and setting people free to live good lives.

Praying

Lord Jesus,
as we get ready for Christmas
help us to know who you are
so we can welcome you
into our lives.
Amen.

Activities

The Christmas landscape continues. Today we are making the star, and fixing it above the house they choose in Bethlehem. Instructions and outlines are on the sheet. The children will need glue and glitter, two lengths of stick and some cotton each.

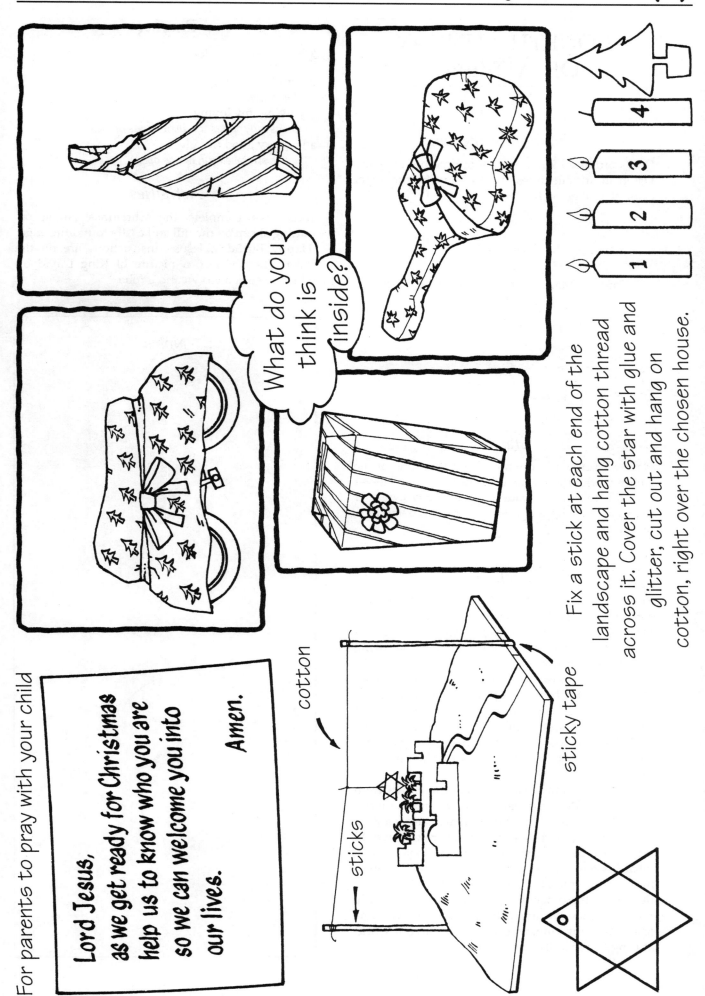

What do you think is inside?

Fix a stick at each end of the landscape and hang cotton thread across it. Cover the star with glue and glitter, cut out and hang on cotton, right over the chosen house.

cotton

sticks

sticky tape

For parents to pray with your child

Lord Jesus,
as we get ready for Christmas
help us to know who you are
so we can welcome you into
our lives.
                                    Amen.

FOURTH SUNDAY OF ADVENT

Thought for the day

God's promised kingdom, announced both to King David in ancient times and to Mary by the angel Gabriel, will go on for ever.

Readings

2 Samuel 7, 1-11, 16
Canticle: Magnificat or Psalm 89:1-4, 19-26
Romans 16:25-27
Luke 1:26-38

Aim

To prepare for King Jesus coming into the world.

Starter

Have a cardboard crown and put it on one of the children who then leads the others to do whatever they do (follow my leader). Swap the crown over till everyone who wants to has a turn at being king or queen.

Teaching

Put the crown on one child's head, and a kingly robe round their shoulders. Once there was a famous king of Israel called King David. He loved God and was a very good king. King David had been born in a city you might have heard of. It was the city of Bethlehem! King David was not brought up in a palace. (Take out a toy sheep and hold it.) He was brought up as a shepherd boy on the hills near Bethlehem, where he helped to look after the sheep. He grew up strong and good, and looking after the people as their king.

(Get out a shiny star, and take the crown from King David. Place the star, the crown and the sheep on the floor together.) Many years later another baby was born in the city of Bethlehem who would grow up to be a king and a shepherd. Do you know what his name was? It was Jesus! (Place a Christmas card or picture showing the Nativity on the floor with the other things.) And as we get ready for Christmas we are getting ready to welcome Jesus, the baby king, who was born into our world at King David's city of Bethlehem.

Praying

Lord Jesus, my King,
  (bow head)
to you I will bring
  (kneel down)
my living, my loving,
  (arms out, palms up, then hands on heart)
and every good thing!
  (arms stretched up, hands open)

Activities

Today we complete the Christmas landscape, putting sheep on the hill and a title round the edge: 'Happy Birthday, Jesus!' Instructions are on the sheet. There is also a picture of King David on which to stick a crown and a robe.

Notes

For parents to pray with your child

Lord Jesus, my King,
(bow head)
to you I will bring
(kneel down)

my living, my loving,
(arms out, palms up, then
hands on heart)
and every good thing!
(arms stretched up, hands open)

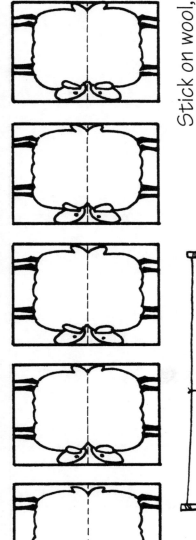

Stick on wool,
cut out and
fold like this

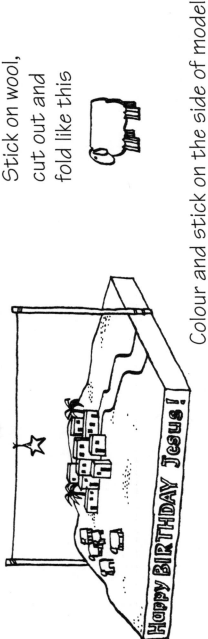

Colour and stick on the side of model

Happy BIRTHDAY Jesus!

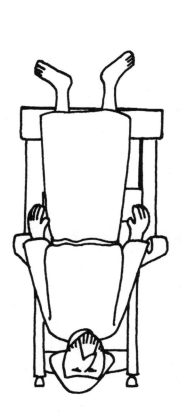

Happy BIRTHDAY Jesus!

CHRISTMAS

CHRISTMAS DAY

Thought for the day

Jesus Christ, the world's Saviour, is here with us, born as a human baby.

Readings

Isaiah 62:6-12
Psalm 97
Titus 3:4-7
Luke 2:(1-7) 8-20

Activities

Christmas Day is very much a time for all God's children to worship together.

Involve all the children in the singing and playing of carols, and in the other ministries of welcoming, serving, collection of gifts and so on. Have nativity toys for the very young to play with, such as knitted Mary, Joseph and Jesus, sheep and shepherds.

I have included a drawing and colouring activity for today so that the children in church can work at this during the sermon.

Notes

First Sunday of Christmas

Thought for the day

Just as the angels said, a Saviour has been born for us.

Readings

Isaiah 61:10-62:3
Psalm 148
Galatians 4:4-7
Luke 2:15-21

Aim

To know that when Jesus was born the shepherds came to welcome him.

Starter

Put stickers of different colours on the children, so that there are at least two of each colour used. They dance and jump around until the music stops. Call out a colour, and those wearing that colour sticker come and shake hands, and greet one another by name – 'Hi, Mazin', 'Wotcha, Will!' Then back to the dancing.

Teaching

Have a crib scene set up somewhere in the room, and dress one child up as an angel. Talk about going to visit people at Christmas – perhaps some of them got in a car or went on a bus or train to visit family or friends, or perhaps some of them had visitors coming to see them. Were there any babies in the places they went?

Today we are going to look at some of the visitors the baby Jesus had, soon after he was born.

In a circle, pretend you are all shepherds, sitting out on the hills under the night sky, round a warm fire. Wrap your cloaks around you, and warm your hands at the fire, getting nice and close to keep cosy. All around us the sheep are bleating. (All make some faraway and nearby bleats.) Look up at all the stars and try to count them . . . oh, there are too many to count, but isn't it beautiful to see the stars shining!

But what's that light in the sky? It's so bright, and it seems to be all around us! (All shrink away from the light, putting your hands up to shield your eyes.) And there's an angel, here on our ordinary hillside! (The child dressed as an angel comes and stands near the group, arms raised.)

The angel said to the shepherds, 'Don't be afraid!' (The angel says, 'Don't be afraid!') All start to relax a bit and get ready to listen to the angel's message. Go into narrative mode and explain that the angel told the shepherds that he had some wonderful news to tell them. A Saviour has just been born in their town of Bethlehem, and they are invited to go and visit him. They'll find him easily because he's wrapped up and lying in the straw in a stable.

The shepherds all look at one another with their eyes open wide in surprise. Just then lots of other angels fill the sky all around them (all look up and point at them), and they're all singing God's praises for all they're worth! (We could all join in – 'Glory to God, glory to God, glory to the Father.')

Then the brightness started to fade away, and the shepherds were sitting in the starry night, rubbing their eyes to make sure they weren't dreaming. But they all remembered the light and the angels and the singing, didn't they? (All look at one another, agreeing.)

Now you're back to being a shepherd again. Suggest that you all go and see if you can find this baby who is God's Son. In a stable in Bethlehem, didn't the angel say? Are we ready, then? (Lead the group of shepherds across to the crib and kneel around it.)

Praying

Jesus, like the shepherds,
we want to welcome you
and thank you for being born.
We love you, Jesus!
Amen.

Activities

On the sheet there is the stable in Bethlehem and the shepherds' hillside to colour in. The children can then draw in a winding road (following the dots, or with these blanked out as you wish) and walk their fingers from the hills to the stable.

Notes

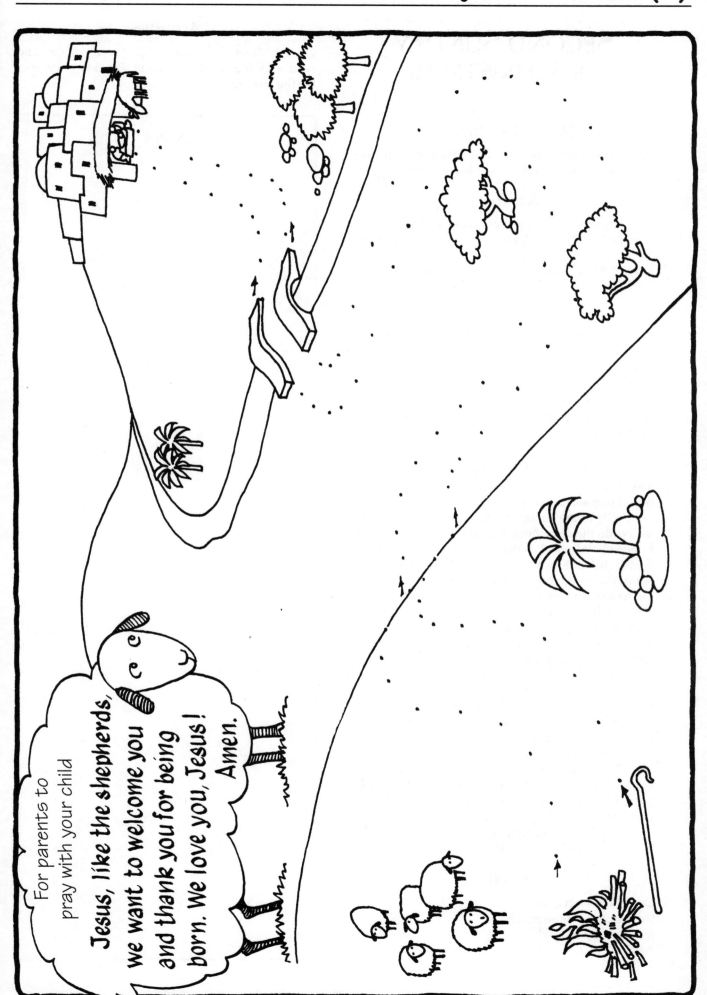

For parents to
pray with your child

Jesus, like the shepherds, we want to welcome you and thank you for being born. We love you, Jesus! Amen.

SECOND SUNDAY OF CHRISTMAS

Thought for the day

The Word made flesh at Christmas was always with God, always expressing his creative love.

Readings

Jeremiah 31:7-14 or Ecclesiasticus 24:1-12
Psalm 147:12-20 or Canticle: Wisdom of Solomon 10:15-21
Ephesians 1:3-14; John 1:(1-9) 10-18

Aim

To know that Jesus is God saying, 'I love you!'

Starter

Collect some model cars and trucks (sized to suit the children in your group) and sit everyone down, spread out. Let them whizz the cars from one to another across the spaces.

Teaching

Talk about how we can send a car off to reach a friend (demonstrate with one car to a child on the other side of the circle) and they can send it back to us. We do the same thing with messages. I can think to myself, 'Mmm, I'd like to thank the children for putting the cars away so nicely', and all I have to do is say the words out loud (say them out loud) and the message races across to your ears! Hands up if you caught the message. Clever, isn't it?

(You could have one or two children sending out a message, and the rest of you catching the spoken message with your ears.)

You can't see those messages, can you? But you can hear them. Some messages you *can* see. What's this one? (Show the road sign for a school.) And this? (Show a green man sign.) That time you caught the message with your eyes.

At Christmas God sent us a very important message. The message looked like this. (Show a picture of the Nativity.) And it meant this. (Show a red heart with the words 'I love you' on it, and read them out.)

Jesus is God's message of love. Jesus is God saying, 'I love you!' (All join in.)

Praying

Dear God, I am glad
that you love us so much.
It makes me happy!
Amen.

Activities

On the sheet they can match the messages and send a loving one to someone. Provide envelopes for the messages.

Notes

Dear_____
Thank you for being
my friend.
Love from

_____

For parents to pray with your child

Dear God,
I am glad that you love us so much.
It makes me happy!
Amen.

WASHING MACHINE REPAIRS

Match the messages

EPIPHANY

THE EPIPHANY

Thought for the day

Jesus, the promised Messiah, is shown to the Gentile world.

Readings

Isaiah 60:1-6
Psalm 72:(1-9) 10-15
Ephesians 3:1-12
Matthew 2:1-12

Aim

To know that the wise men brought presents to Jesus.

Starter

Fix a star on to a stick and give it to one of the children. Wherever this child goes with the star, the others follow. If the star stops, everyone stops. Swap the star around until everyone who wants to lead has had a go.

Teaching

On a long strip of lining paper or wallpaper draw some hills and a starry sky, based on the picture below. Lay the sheet out in front of the children, and have at the ready a shiny star and a cut-out picture of the wise men. The smaller you make these the longer the journey will look.

Who do we know who followed a star? Yes, it was the wise men from many miles away. They followed a great bright star in the sky which was moving, night by night. (Move the star as you speak, and then make the wise men walk after it to catch it up.) The star went on like this for nights and nights, until at last it stopped. (Stop the star over the town of Bethlehem.) And the wise men followed it all the way to a town called Bethlehem. Who did they find at Bethlehem? They found Jesus there. (Place a Christmas card of Joseph, Mary and Jesus on the city of Bethlehem.)

What did they do when they found Jesus? (Swap the Christmas card for one showing the wise men giving their presents.) They treated Jesus as if he was a little king. They bowed and knelt in front of him, and gave him the presents they had brought.

What were the presents? There was gold (lay down something gold – preferably real gold if practical! If you are wearing a gold ring you can

take it off and place it down, which says a lot about real giving without a word spoken) . . . frankincense (again the real thing is ideal, so they can smell what it's like) . . . and myrrh (the Body Shop sells it, or use any spicy ointment and let them rub a bit into their skin if they want to).

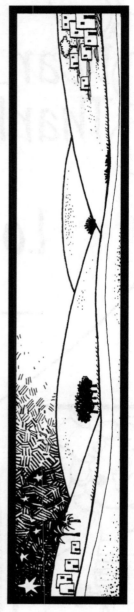

Praying

Jesus, can you guess
   (*pretend to hide a present behind your back*)
what I have brought
to give you?
It's ME!
   (*bring hands out and hold them up and out, as you jump forward*)

Activities

There is an activity to match objects with their silhouettes, and a picture to colour of the wise men giving their presents.

You can colour this picture of the wise men giving Jesus their presents

Match the toy with its shadow

For parents to pray with your child

Jesus, can you guess what I have brought to give you?   [pretend to hide a present behind your back]

[bring hands out and hold them up and out, as you jump forward]

It's ME!

THE BAPTISM OF CHRIST: FIRST SUNDAY OF EPIPHANY

Thought for the day

Through the Holy Spirit, Jesus is affirmed at his Baptism as God's beloved Son, and we too are given the Spirit of God which affirms us as God's adopted daughters and sons.

Readings

Genesis 1:1-5
Psalm 29
Acts 19:1-7
Mark 1:4-11

Aim

To know what baptism is.

Starter

Have a time of water play. To cut down on mess, protect the floor with plastic sheeting (plastic table-cloths are good for this job) and have several washing-up bowls with a lowish level of water in them. Gather an assortment of containers, tea strainers and funnels to play with.

Teaching

Talk about playing in the water at a swimming pool, on the beach or by a river, and what the water looks, sounds and feels like. What is it like under the water? What happens to dirty things when they're washed in water?

When people promise to spend their life following Jesus, they are washed in water in church, and given their name. It's called being baptised, or Christened. (Talk about the font in your church, and any baptisms they remember, and show some pictures of people being baptised.)

Today we remember when Jesus was baptised in the river Jordan. He waded into the water and John the Baptist (who was Jesus' cousin) dipped him right under the water. When he came up, all wet, he heard God, his Father, saying to him, 'You are my Son and I love you. I am very pleased with you.'

Praying

Lord God,
I am one of your children.
I belong to you!
Amen.

Activities

Have some strips of blue and silver wool, paper or cloth which the children can stick on to the picture of Jesus' baptism for the water in the river Jordan. A reminder of their own baptism can be made using the outline provided, and more water-coloured wool or string.

Notes

24

First Sunday of Epiphany (B)

- Colour yourself in.
- Thread blue and silver wool through the holes and fix with tape.

Stick on wool, cellophane or cloth to be the water.

For parents to pray with your child

Lord God,
I am one of
your children.
I belong to you!
Amen.

SECOND SUNDAY OF EPIPHANY

Thought for the day

Jesus, the Christ, unlocks the mysteries of God.

Readings

1 Samuel 3:1-10 (11-20)
Psalm 139:1-6, 13-18
Revelation 5:1-10
John 1:43-51

Aim

To know that Jesus shows us what God is like.

Starter

Cut up a magic painting book and supply clean water and brushes, so the children can watch a coloured picture emerging. Alternatively, draw simple pictures (like a sun or a house) on white paper with a candle and let the children paint a colour wash over them to reveal the pictures.

Teaching

Talk about how we couldn't at first see the colours or the pictures, but they were there, hidden, waiting for us to find them.

We can't see God, either. That doesn't mean God isn't there; it means he is there hidden from our sight. We can look around us, up into the sky and down into the deep seas, and know God must be very clever and important to make all this.

But the one who most explains to us what God is like is Jesus.

What is Jesus like? He loves people, whoever they are, however poor or rich they are, and however young or old they are. He helps them, makes them better and chats with them. He is a good friend. He never lets anyone down. He forgives people even when they are really nasty to him.

The more we get to know Jesus, the more we will be finding out about what God is like.

Praying

Thank you, Jesus,
for showing us
what God is like.

Activities

On the sheet there is space for the children to draw an invisible picture with a candle or a white crayon. They can then take this home for someone else to make visible by painting. Also there are some pictures which help them state what they know about God.

Notes

Jesus shows us what God is like

What do I know about God

1. Draw an invisible picture here!

Thank you, Jesus, for showing us what God is like.

2. Paint a colour wash over here to see the hidden picture!

THIRD SUNDAY OF EPIPHANY

Thought for the day

Signs of glory lead us to believe in Jesus as Lord and Saviour.

Readings

Genesis 14:17-20
Psalm 128
Revelation 19:6-10
John 2:1-11

Aim

To know we can follow the signs to find out who God is.

Starter

A treasure trail in pictures. Prepare simple drawings of different places in the room and number them. Keep number 1 yourself, and place number 2 in the place shown on number 1. Continue placing all the pictures until at the last place (pictured in the previous number) you put the treasure – enough sweets/stickers/crayons for everyone. Start off by showing everyone the first picture, which sends them off to where the second one is lurking, and so on until they are led to the treasure.

Teaching

Talk about how we were led to the treasure bit by bit, and not straightaway. Each clue led us a little closer.

What things can help us to find out who Jesus is?

Have a candle, some water and a toy sheep all hidden separately under cloths or tea towels. Explain that hidden here we've got some things which can lead us to find out who Jesus is and what he is like.

Uncover the candle. What can a candle tell us about Jesus? Light the candle as you explain that a candle is a living flame of light in the darkness; it helps us see, so we don't trip over things, and it shows things up clearly. And that's what Jesus does. He is the light of love and goodness shining in the darkness of all that is wrong and bad. He helps us see the right way to live so we don't waste our lives hating and spoiling.

Uncover the water. What can water tell us about Jesus? Water is clear and clean, it washes, and when we are thirsty it takes our thirst away. And that's what Jesus does. We can always trust him because he is always honest with us, he forgives us when we are sorry for making others unhappy, and he is like a drink when you're thirsty – very nice!

Uncover the sheep. What can a sheep tell us about Jesus? Sheep need a shepherd, and so do we. Jesus is like a good shepherd who looks after us and leads us safely through our whole life.

Praying

Left, right, left, right,
we are walking your way, Jesus.
Left, right, left, right,
that's the way to go!
Left, right, left, right,
we are walking your way, Jesus.
Left, right, left, right,
Let the loving show!

Activities

There is a tangled lines activity to discover which line leads them to the treasure, and instructions for making a shoe imprint on foil so they can match up the print with the sole of the shoe they are wearing. Each child will need a shoe-sized piece of foil, and the group will need newspaper, a folded cloth and either a normal damp patch of ground, snow or a damp washing-up bowl.

Notes

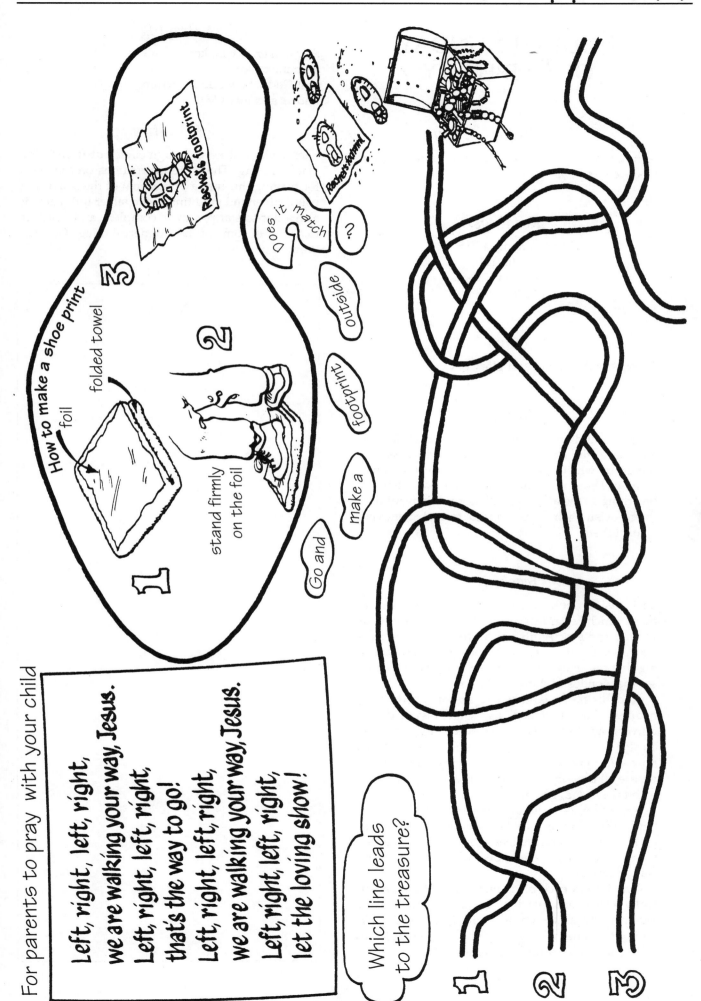

For parents to pray with your child

Left, right, left, right,
we are walking your way, Jesus.
Left, right, left, right,
that's the way to go!
Left, right, left, right,
we are walking your way, Jesus.
Left, right, left, right,
let the loving show!

Which line leads to the treasure?

How to make a shoe print

foil

folded towel

stand firmly on the foil

Rachel's footprint

Rachel's footprint

Does it match ?

Go and make a footprint outside

1 2 3

FOURTH SUNDAY OF EPIPHANY

Thought for the day

Jesus displays all the signs that mark him out to be God's chosen One.

Readings

Deuteronomy 18:15-20
Psalm 111
Revelation 12:1-5a
Mark 1:21-28

Aim

To explore the power and glory of God.

Starter

Take the children outside to look up at the sky and wonder at the clouds and the stars which are out there but which we can't see because the sun is shining. Draw their attention to the way they are breathing in the air that is all around them, and let them swish their arms around to feel it moving against them.

Teaching

Back inside, look at our hands and the skin on them which keeps our insides together, protects us so well and exactly fits us! All the things we have been looking at are the work of someone so amazing that our eyes can't even see him – we can only see the wonderful things he has made.

And his name is God. We are only alive here because God invented us. God invented the universe we live in. God sees everything that goes on. He is watching us now. He is listening to us now – not just to what we're saying, but to what we are all thinking as well! He hears us feeling sad when we're sad, grumpy when we're grumpy, and happy when we're happy. He knows when we try hard to be kind, even when we don't really want to. He knows when we feel sorry for someone and want to help them. He knows when we are being silly or unkind.

God knows each of us and every other person really well, even if we don't know that much about him yet. But as we get to know God more, we'll find out that he is completely good and completely loving as well as completely powerful.

Praying

Star maker, sky maker,
help me to see
that God who made everything
knows and loves ME!

Activities

Each child will need a large circle cut from half a black bin bag. There are instructions on the sheet for turning this into a prayer mat of the starry sky, using silver and gold tinsel, and silver foil. There is also a star-to-star picture to complete, and a picture to colour of some of the wonderful things God has thought of.

Notes

Join the stars to make a star!

Here are some of the lovely things God has thought of ....

Stick on shiny stars and planets to make your starry sky prayer mat. Then you can stand on it to praise God!

For parents to pray with your child

Star maker, sky maker, help me to see that God who made everything knows and loves ME!

Large black plastic circle (from bin bag)

ORDINARY TIME

PROPER 1

Sunday between 3 and 9 February inclusive
(if earlier than the Second Sunday before Lent)

Thought for the day

The good news about God is far too good to keep to ourselves.

Readings

Isaiah 40:12-31
Psalm 147:1-11, 20c
1 Corinthians 9:16-23
Mark 1:29-39

Aim

To look at how they can spread the good news of God's love.

Starter

Distribute the contents of a tube of Smarties around the group, or spread some slices of bread with butter and jam to make small sandwiches to give out at coffee time after church.

Teaching

Start with a news time, encouraging the children to share any good news they have, so that everyone can enjoy the good things with them.

The good news we all have to share is that our God is fantastic! Think together about some of the things about God which are wonderful and good.

Not everyone knows these things yet. Quite a lot of people don't know much about God at all, or they don't know how lovely and kind and loving he is. Point out that it seems a great pity that they don't yet know and we do – so how can we let them know our good news about God?

We can use our eyes (everyone points to their eyes) to notice when people need cheering up, or when they need some help, or when they need a hug, just as God notices our needs. We can use our ears (point to ears) to listen carefully, as God listens carefully to us. We can use our mouths (point to them) to speak words that are kind and friendly, and we can tell people about God. And we can use our hands (show them) to do things for people that are kind and loving and helpful.

Praying

I'm not going to keep it a secret – Shh!
I'M GOING TO SHOUT IT LOUD!
GOD IS REAL!
GOD'S THE ONE WHO MADE US ALL
AND GOD'S THE ONE WHO LOVES US ALL!

Activities

On the sheet there are pictures of different things to shout about, and they can work out what the good news is in each case. There is also a picture to colour of all kinds of people happy and dancing because they have just found out that God loves them all.

Notes

What's the news?

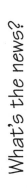

What's the news?

GOD Loves us all !

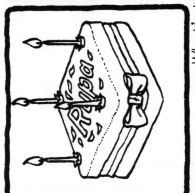

What's the news?

For parents to pray with your child

I'm not going to keep it
a secret – Shh!
I'M GOING TO SHOUT IT
LOUD! GOD IS REAL!
GOD'S THE ONE WHO MADE
US ALL AND GOD'S THE
ONE WHO LOVES US ALL!

PROPER 2

Sunday between 10 and 16 February inclusive
(if earlier than the Second Sunday before Lent)

Thought for the day

Jesus wants to heal us to wholeness, and to him no one is untouchable.

Readings

2 Kings 5:1-14
Psalm 30
1 Corinthians 9:24-27
Mark 1:40-45

Aim

To know that God enjoys helping us and making us better.

Starter

Cut out a number of spots of different colours (about 30 centimetres across) and spread them out on the floor. All round the room are placed small spots of the same colours, and the children go round spotting the spots and placing them on the matching large spot on the floor.

Teaching

Sometimes we get spots when we're ill. Does anyone remember having spots? (With chicken pox, for instance.) Today we are going to meet someone whose skin was covered in white spots because he had a skin illness. The man's name was Naaman.

Spread out carpet tiles or a couple of large towels on the floor and tell the story from 2 Kings 5:1-14 in your own words, using cut-out pictures of the characters based on the drawings below.

Praying

Dear Father God,
we pray for all the people
who are ill,
and for those who are looking after them.
Amen.

Activities

Using the sheet the children can cut out a Naaman and dip him seven times in the river. There is also a series of pictures of the story to place in order and colour in.

Notes

For parents to pray with your child

Dear Father God, we pray for all the people who are ill, and for those who are looking after them.

Amen.

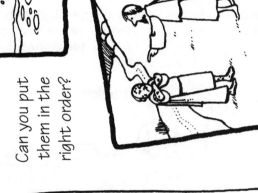

1234567

Dip Naaman in the water **7** times

Colour and cut out

Can you put them in the right order?

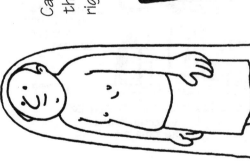

Fold

Cut slit

Fold

Colour this blue

PROPER 3

Sunday between 17 and 23 February inclusive
(if earlier than the Second Sunday before Lent)

Thought for the day

The Son of Man has authority on earth to forgive sins.

Readings

Isaiah 43:18-25; Psalm 41
2 Corinthians 1:18-22; Mark 2:1-12

Aim

To know the story of the man let down through the roof.

Starter

Construct a pulley as shown in the diagram below, and let everyone help load the bricks that are on the top of our building down to the ground, taking it in turns to do the winding.

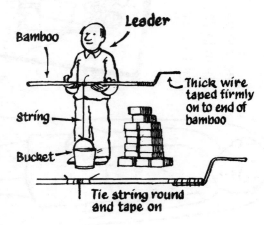

Teaching

In our story today, four friends were lowering something down from the roof on to the ground below – like we were, but it wasn't bricks!

Use a prototype model from the worksheet, made from a shoe box as shown, and tell the children the story of today's Gospel as you act it out with the working model.

Praying

Thank you for the friends
who brought us to you, Jesus.
And thank you for legs to run with!
(Run)
Amen.

Activities

Each child will need a cardboard box to make the model of the house. Have the hole in the roof already cut. They will also need some tape or wool to place under the man to lower him down through the roof, and plasticene or modelling clay to make the man.

Notes

3. Colour the people, cut them out and stick them in the house

in the house

in the house

on the roof

on the roof

For parents to pray with your child

Thank you for the friends who brought us to you, Jesus. And thank you for legs to run with! (Run) Amen.

You can lower the man down through the roof

1. Make the man who can't move out of plasticine

2. Cut out this bed. Stick tape here and here

SECOND SUNDAY BEFORE LENT

Thought for the day

Christ is the image of the unseen God.

Readings

Proverbs 8:1, 22-31
Psalm 104:24-35
Colossians 1:15-20
John 1:1-14

Aim

To delight, like God's wisdom, in all creation.

Starter

Prepare a selection of smells and textures for the children to sample. Here are some suggestions:

- incense sticks or essential oils of different fragrances

- primroses and daffodils

- fruits and vegetables

- bark, new and crackly leaves, shells, feathers and stones

- different textured fabrics

Teaching

Gather round all the objects and talk with the children about the ones they specially like, enjoying the variety. We have all been born into this beautiful world, with all its colours and shapes to look at and enjoy. Go through different categories of what there is, so that they can think of examples of them all (for example, round, red, yellow, prickly, shiny, rough and smooth, quiet and loud, quick and slow, little and big, and things that are invisible and hidden). What a loving God it must be who thought of all this and gave us such a lovely planet to live on!

Praying

All that we can hear and everything we can see,
including me,
we all of us spring from God,
who cares for each of us unendingly.
Let the whole earth sing of his love!

Activities

Have ready plenty of glue, and an assortment of small examples of things that are shiny, colourful, tasty, soft and round, so that they can choose things to stick on to the appropriate spaces on the sheet. There is music to go with today's prayer (see page 128), which the children can sing as they hold up their finished 'samplers'.

Notes

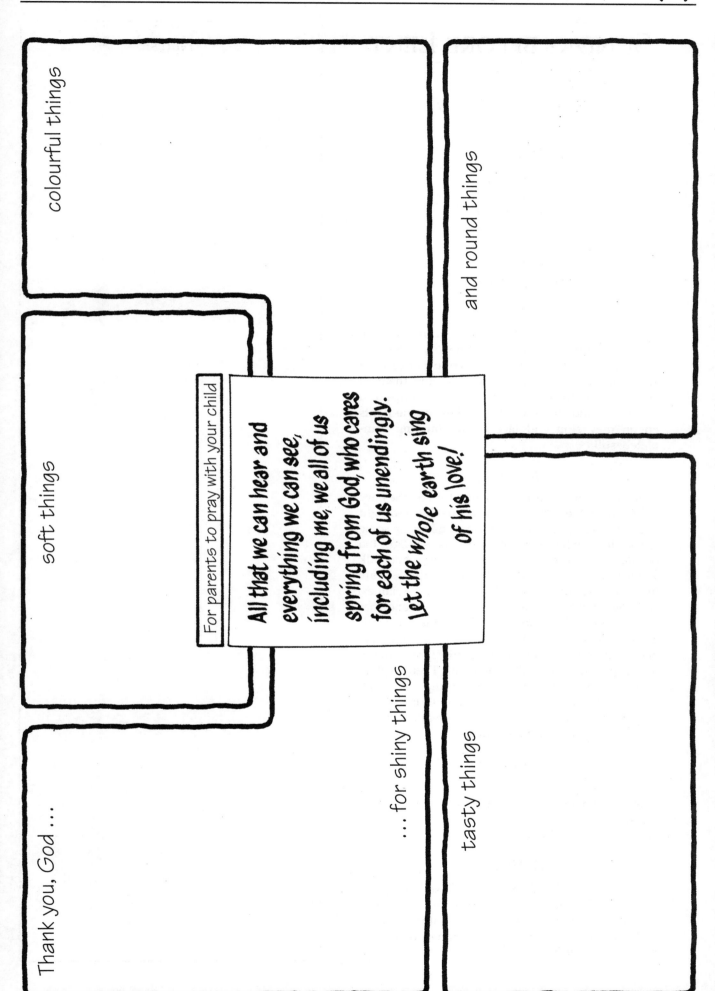

colourful things

and round things

soft things

For parents to pray with your child

All that we can hear and
everything we can see,
including me, we all of us
spring from God, who cares
for each of us unendingly.
Let the whole earth sing
of his love!

... for shiny things

tasty things

Thank you, God ...

SUNDAY BEFORE LENT

Thought for the day

God's glory shows.

Readings

2 Kings 2:1-12
Psalm 50:1-6
2 Corinthians 4:3-6
Mark 9:2-9

Aim

To sense God's glory and holiness.

Starter

Use a set of Christmas tree lights, strung across a notice board or round a door frame. If you haven't access to any fairy lights, bring a couple of bedside lamps and a multisocket, so you can turn them all on and off from one switch. Everyone jumps and dances around the room, but whenever the lights go on they stop and face them, standing completely still.

Teaching

When everyone is sitting in a circle, turn on the fairy lights, make the room as dark as possible and light some candles, standing them on a mirror or some foil so that the lights are reflected. As you light the candles have some quiet music playing, and talk about how good light is, and how beautiful. Draw the children's attention to the colour of the flames, and the bright reflections. Remind everyone that God is here with us, and he loves us and our families very much. For a short while, encourage everyone to sit here very still in the candlelight with the music playing, in God's company. Then explain how we often think of God as being like light, because he is so full of goodness and loveliness. The prayer can be sung (to the tune of *See-saw, Marjorie Daw*) as you sit around the candles.

Praying

Jesus, Jesus,
Lord of earth and heaven,
Jesus, Jesus,
Lord of earth and heaven!

Activities

The sheet can be turned into a stained glass window by colouring the outline with wax crayons, and then sponging a little cooking oil over it. Leave to dry out, and the paper will have become translucent.

Notes

For parents to pray with your child

(To the tune of see-saw,
Marjorie Daw)
Jesus, Jesus,
Lord of earth and heaven,
Jesus, Jesus,
Lord of earth and heaven!

Colour the
window with wax
crayons.
Sponge on a little oil.
See the colours light
up as the sun shines
through!

LENT

FIRST SUNDAY OF LENT

Thought for the day

After his Baptism Jesus is led by the Spirit into the wilderness before returning to proclaim God's kingdom.

Readings

Genesis 9:8-17
Psalm 25:1-10
1 Peter 3:18-22
Mark 1:9-15

Aim

To know the story of Noah, the flood and the rainbow.

Starter

Put stickers of different colours on the children and stand in a circle, holding hands to make archways. When you hold up a colour, the child wearing that colour sticker runs in and out of the archways, round the circle and back to their place. Whenever you hold up a picture of a rainbow, the whole circle joins hands and comes in to the middle and out again, shouting, 'God loves us!'

Teaching

Spread out carpet tiles or a large sheet on the ground and sit around it. Use cut-outs, based on the pictures below to tell the story of Noah and the flood. Animals can be models if you prefer. The children can help move the characters around. Bring out the way God rescued Noah and his family and kept them safe, and how the rainbow is a sign of God's love that will never let us down.

Praying

(This can be sung to the tune of *One, two, three four five, once I caught a fish alive*)

Violet, indigo and blue –
God loves me, that's always true.
Green, yellow, orange, red –
that is what the rainbow said!

Activities

The sheet can be turned into a rainbow mobile. The children will need lengths of different coloured wool, glue sticks and cotton, and you may prefer to copy the sheet on to thicker paper than usual.

For parents to pray with your child

Violet, indigo and blue –
God loves me, that's always true.
Green, yellow, orange, red –
that is what the rainbow said!

Colour, stick on
wool to rainbow
and hang up like this

SECOND SUNDAY OF LENT

Thought for the day

A commitment of faith has far-reaching implications.

Readings

Genesis 17:1-7, 15-16
Psalm 22:23-31
Romans 4:13-25
Mark 8:31-38

Aim

To know that we can trust God.

Starter

Sit in a circle and show the children the items mentioned as you ask them to decide which of the two they would trust:

* Which would you trust to sit on – a chair or a balloon?

* Which would you trust to build a house with – bricks or sponges?

* Which would you trust to swing on – cotton or a rope?

* Which would you choose to carry your packed lunch in – an airtight box or an envelope?

Teaching

We trust things that we think will work well – things that won't let us down. And we trust people who love us, because we know they will be wanting us to be safe and happy. We can't trust strangers, because we don't know if they are wanting us to be safe and happy or not. Use a parent and a child puppet to act this out. First the child is scared of riding a new bike, but the parent reassures them that they will be holding them so they will be safe. The child agrees to try, as the parent has promised to make sure they don't fall. Then the child wants to ride on the main road, but the parent explains they can't because it's too dangerous. The child reluctantly agrees, knowing that the parent is wanting them to be safe because they are loved.

God is like a loving parent to all of us – God loves us and wants us to be safe and happy for always, in this life and after we die. So we can trust God completely. He will never do anything bad or wrong. He will never let us down. He is always there, watching over us and loving us.

Praying

Jesus, we know we can trust you –
you love us
and will never let us down.
Amen.

Activities

The teaching on trust is continued on the sheet, with some thinking to do about what we are prepared to trust and why. There is also a picture of some people in dangerous places, and they can experience being on the caring end by noticing needs and providing the necessary help by drawing it in.

Notes

THIRD SUNDAY OF LENT

Thought for the day

God's wisdom may shock us. Jesus, obedient to God's Law and fulfilling it, dies a death which, according to the Law, makes him cursed.

Readings

Exodus 20:1-17; Psalm 19
1 Corinthians 1:18-25; John 2:13-22

Aim

To know Jesus' summary of the Law.

Starter

Traffic lights. Prepare three coloured circles – red, amber and green. Explain that to play this game we have to obey the rules. When the green is shown, everyone jumps and dances around the room. When amber (or yellow) is shown, everyone gets ready to stop. When red is shown, everyone stops quite still. When red and amber are shown together, everyone gets ready to move again.

Teaching

Praise them for obeying the rules so well. That meant we could all enjoy playing the game together. It's very useful to have rules. Some rules are there to keep us safe (like not playing in the road), and some are to make sure that things are done fairly (like queuing up for rides at a theme park).

Jesus gave us two good rules to help us live our lives really well, and we're going to learn them today. As we've got two hands each we can use our hands to help us learn the rules.

Demonstrate raising one hand to heaven as you say, 'Love God', and then stretching the other hand out, palm up, as you say, 'Love one another'. Then everyone can try it a couple of times. The rules can also be written on two balloons with an OHP pen, and the balloons inflated. Any of the children who now think they can say the two rules on their own can do that in front of the others. (Everyone will benefit from the reinforcement, and the children enjoy being able to do it well.)

Now we've learnt God's two rules, all we have to do is live by them! Each day we can think over what we've done and ask ourselves, 'How have we been loving God today? And how have we been loving one another today?' And the next day we can try and do it even better!

Praying

(Say the prayer with actions.)

Love God, love one another,
that's the way to live.
Love God, love one another,
happy to forgive.

Activities

There is a picture on the sheet with children and adults of all ages. The children can pick out all the loving God and loving one another that is going on. Part of the sheet can be made into wrist bands with the two rules on, which the children can decorate and wear.

Notes

For parents to pray with your child

Love God, love one another,
that's the way to live.
Love God, love one another,
happy to forgive.

Colour the wrist bands and fix them round your wrists with sticky tape or staples.

Me, being kind and loving

LOVE ONE ANOTHER

LOVE GOD

Can you spot all the loving?

Love God, love one another

FOURTH SUNDAY OF LENT: MOTHERING SUNDAY

Thought for the day

God provides comfort in all our troubles and sufferings.

Readings

Exodus 2:1-10 or 1 Samuel 1:20-28
Psalm 34:11-20 or Psalm 127:1-4
2 Corinthians 1:3-7 or Colossians 3:12-17
Luke 2:33-35 or John 19:25-27

Activities

Today is not one for learning separately but for celebrating and learning together. Involve the children and young people in the music group or choir, as servers, welcomers, collectors for the offering, and so on. Provide shakers and bells for the younger ones to play during one or two hymns, and streamers to wave. Gather the children round the altar for the eucharistic prayer and choose hymns where the language is accessible.

Have materials for making flowers available for the younger children. The activity sheet should be enlarged to A3 size if possible.

Notes

Colour both sides of the card. Cut them out, stick them together and fold

FIFTH SUNDAY OF LENT

Thought for the day

Through Christ's death, full life would come to people of all nations and generations.

Readings

Jeremiah 31:31-34
Psalm 51:1-12 or Psalm 119:9-16
Hebrews 5:5-10
John 12:20-33

Aim

To know that Jesus loves us enough to help us even when it hurts.

Starter

Play shops, with cartons, fruit and vegetables for sale and toy money, so that they get the idea of there being cost and payment.

Teaching

Talk about their shopping, and bring out a carrier bag from a local supermarket, with some cheap and expensive items in it. Talk together about which don't cost very much, and which cost a lot. Mention other things which cost lots and lots of money, like houses and holidays. We have to save up for things like that. Sometimes we see a toy or a game we would like, but we don't think it's worth all the money, so we choose not to get it. (Or Mum and Dad say that!)

There was something that Jesus wanted very, very much. It wasn't a toy, and it wasn't something to eat or wear. What Jesus really wanted was to save the world. He wanted us all to be happy and free. But how much would it cost? It couldn't be bought with money. It could only be bought with his life.

Jesus thought about it. He wondered if it was really worth giving up his life so we could be happy and free. He knew that giving up his life would hurt. A lot.

But remember, Jesus loves us very much. He loves us so much that he decided he was even willing to give up his life so we could be free and happy. He thought it was worth the cost of all that hurt. So he did it, and that's why we can be happy and free!

Praying

(Sing this to the tune of *Frère Jacques*, with the children echoing the leader's words and actions.)

I am dancing, **I am dancing**,
   (dance)
'Thank you, God!' **'Thank you, God!'**
   (clap hands)
I am singing, **I am singing**,
   (sway)
'Thank you, God!' **'Thank you, God!'**
   (clap hands)

Activities

On the sheet there is a purse full of pictures, and some other things which 'cost' the items in the purse. The children choose what they would be willing to give up for the experiences 'on offer'. There is also a 'thank you, Jesus!' hat to make and wear. Have a selection of sparkly and shiny things to decorate it with.

Notes

For parents to pray with your child

(To the tune of Frère Jacques)
YOU   **YOUR CHILD**
I am dancing, (dance)   I am dancing,
'Thank you, God!' (clap)   'Thank you, God!'
I am singing, (sway)   I am singing,
'Thank you, God!' (clap) 'Thank you God!'

GIVING CAN BE HARD FOR US

Thank you, Jesus!

B

Stick on shiny bits of paper to decorate the hat. Stick string to each side (A and B) and tie on child's head.

to give to a child who is too poor to buy pencils for school?

to give to a child who has no toys at all?

to give to a child who is hungry?

... for these ...

Would you part with these ...

Teddy

CHOCOLATE

Some of your pencils

Dinner

PALM SUNDAY

Thought for the day

As the Messiah, Jesus enters Jerusalem, knowing that he rides towards rejection and death in order to save his people.

Readings

Liturgy of the Palms:
Mark 11:1-11 or John 12:12-16
Psalm 118:1-2, 19-24

Liturgy of the Passion:
Isaiah 50:4-9a
Psalm 31:9-16
Philippians 2:5-11
Mark 14:1-15:47 or Mark 15:1-39 (40-47)

Aim

To know that Jesus came into Jerusalem, welcomed and cheered by all the people.

Starter

If possible, let the children join in with the all-age procession, playing their instruments, dancing and singing as they go. Or gather all the age groups and take them on a Palm Sunday procession, preferably outside. Take a portable tape player so they can all sing along with the songs.

Teaching

Show a picture or a model of a donkey. There's a donkey in our story today. He was just an ordinary donkey, and a young one, but he was given a very important job to do.

Tell the children the story of Jesus' entry into Jerusalem from the donkey's point of view. Bring in what the donkey saw and heard and felt and smelt, and how pleased and proud he felt to have his friend Jesus riding on his back. If you prefer to have a 'script', Palm Tree Bible Stories have it written from the donkey's perspective in *Jesus on a donkey*, and Nan Goodall's classic, *Donkey's glory* (Mowbray, 1980), includes this special journey.

Praying

(Jingle some keys or bottle tops during this prayer.)

Donkey riding, donkey riding,
hear the children sing!
Donkey riding, donkey riding,
'JESUS IS OUR KING!'

Activities

Pin the tail on the donkey. Use the picture of a donkey and make a tail from some wool, with blutack on the top end. The children shut their eyes (or have them blindfolded) and fix the tail where they reckon it belongs. Using an old sock and some wool they can make a donkey puppet to remind them of today's teaching. (If you don't have any old socks, try the charity shops, or a jumble sale.)

Notes

Cut here

Old grey or brown sock

Stick on ears and wool
Colour on the eyes
Wear on your hand and say the prayer

For parents to pray with your child

Donkey riding, donkey riding,
hear the children sing!
Donkey riding, donkey riding,
'JESUS IS OUR KING!'

(Rattle some keys or bottle tops in a bag)

Two ear shapes cut from the sock

Make a donkey

Colour me then try and put my tail on the right place

EASTER

EASTER DAY

If possible, it is recommended that the children and young people are in church with the other age groups today. Use and adapt some of the all-age ideas from the *Living Stones* Complete Resource Book, and involve the young people in some of the music and in the cleaning and decorating of the church.

Thought for the day

Jesus is alive; Love has won the victory over sin and death.

Readings

Acts 10:34-43 or Isaiah 25:6-9
Psalm 118:1-2, 14-24
1 Corinthians 15:1-11 or Acts 10:34-43
John 20:1-18 or Mark 16:1-8

Aim

To know that Jesus died and is alive again for ever.

Starter

Hide some Easter eggs (outside if possible) and have an Easter egg hunt before distributing them fairly among the children.

Teaching

Look together at some hens' eggs and pictures of chicks, birds and dinosaurs, all coming from eggs. Talk about the springtime and all the signs of new life around at the moment.

Today is Easter Day. It's very special because it's the day we remember Jesus coming to life for ever. Jesus went around doing good and loving people, making them better and helping them get to know what God is like. But some people wanted Jesus out of the way, and he was killed – they nailed him to a big cross. It was very sad, but Jesus went on loving and forgiving even then.

When some of his friends went to the grave on the Sunday morning, they couldn't find his dead body; it wasn't there. Why? Because Jesus wasn't dead any more – he was alive! He would never die again. Jesus is alive for ever! (You could all sing *Jesus' love is very wonderful* to celebrate.)

Praying

Did Jesus die? YES!
Is Jesus dead? NO!
Is he alive again? YES, YES, YES!
JESUS IS ALIVE!

Activities

On the sheet there are pictures of a chick being hatched to put in sequence, and a picture of the Easter garden to colour. This can be stuck on a folded piece of coloured paper and given as an Easter card to the family.

Notes

SECOND SUNDAY OF EASTER

Thought for the day

Our faith in the risen Christ is bound to affect the way we live.

Readings

Acts 4:32-35
Psalm 133
1 John 1:1–2:2
John 20:19-31

Aim

To know that Jesus is with us now.

Starter

Have four different sounds, such as a bell, a drum, a rattle and a whistle. When the children hear the sounds they do the appropriate actions. The bell means 'now clap', the drum 'now jump up and down', the rattle 'now sit', and the whistle 'now smile'.

Teaching

Talk about what we are all doing now. This might be sitting in a circle, listening, folding our arms, breathing, and thinking. Some things, like breathing, we do all the time, and hardly notice. Take a few breaths to notice what goes on day and night, when we're awake and when we're asleep, so that we stay alive. So there's lots going on *now* just in our own body.

What's going on now as well as us sitting in a circle in St Martin's, East Ham? Lots of other groups of Pebbles are sitting in their circles in other churches! (Why not pray for them now – they will be praying for you!) What else is going on now? Think about what is happening at the moment on the roads and in hospitals, and in other countries, where some people are fast asleep and others are going to bed.

We only see our little bit of *now*, but God sees all of it! Jesus is here *now* for all the people and all the places!

Praying

(Loudly) Tick tock, tick tock,
Jesus you are with us NOW!
(Softly) Tick tock, tick tock,
(Very softly) Jesus . . . you are here.

Activities

On the sheet there are pictures of Jesus with us while we're playing, eating, travelling, working. It helps children to have it pictured for them, and then they have no problem in understanding that Jesus is with us even though we can't actually see him. They can colour the pictures and put them around the house at appropriate places to remind them. There is also a 'Jesus is my friend' badge to make.

Notes

THIRD SUNDAY OF EASTER

Thought for the day

Having redeemed us by his death, Jesus can offer us the forgiveness of our sin, which sets us free to live.

Readings

Acts 3:12-19
Psalm 4
1 John 3:1-7
Luke 24:36b-48

Aim

To know that Jesus calms our fears when we're scared.

Starter

What's the time, Mr Wolf? The children creep up on Mr Wolf, asking him the time, and he replies with different times. If he says, 'Dinner time!' the children turn and run as Mr Wolf tries to catch someone.

Teaching

Talk about how mums and dads make us feel safe when we're scared or frightened. Sometimes they make us laugh and show us that we don't need to be frightened. (Like Dad pretending to wear a bib, so the baby sees it as funny instead of scary.) Sometimes they explain so we aren't scared any more because we understand it better. (Like barking being a dog's way of saying hello.) And if something really is frightening, mums and dads make us feel safer just by holding us close to them, or just being there. (You can use parent and baby soft toys to act out these situations.)

Now explain that God is like that with us all. When his disciples were all scared, on the first Easter Day, Jesus came and comforted them. Jesus knows when we're scared, and we can tell him all about it. He will help us to be brave. He works through other people to look after us, and he works through us to look after other people who are scared. So whenever we make someone feel better, or calm their fears, we are working on God's team!

Praying

I will lie down in peace
and sleep;
it is you, Lord,
who keeps me safe.
Amen.

Activities

On the sheet there are some pictures of people who need some help to stop them being frightened, and the children can draw in the things or people they need. The prayer can be hung up in the bedroom to use as a night prayer.

Notes

Mick is frightened of the dark.
Draw in a light for him.

Pip is frightened to be left at nursery school.
Draw in a friend for her.

Can you draw in the things or people they need to stop them being frightened

Don't be afraid! I'm here.

says Jesus

Susie is frightened of riding her new bike.
Draw in some stabilisers for her.

For parents to pray with your child

cut out and hang on the bed

I will lie down in peace and sleep, it is you, Lord, who keeps me safe. Amen.

FOURTH SUNDAY OF EASTER

Thought for the day

'I am the Good Shepherd and I lay down my life for the sheep.'

Readings

Acts 4:5-12
Psalm 23
1 John 3:16-24
John 10:11-18

Aim

To know that Jesus is our Good Shepherd.

Starter

Hunt the sheep. Use a soft toy sheep and take it in turns to hide it while everyone closes their eyes. Then everyone looks for it until it's found again.

Teaching

The children can help you make a landscape of hills, using a large towel draped over some upturned pots and basins, and arranging a few pot plants on it. Wind a long blue scarf between the hills as a stream of water. Place some sheep on the hills. These can either be model or toy ones, or they can be made from the pattern below.

Move the sheep around (the children can make all the sheep and lamb bleating noises) as you tell them how a good shepherd looks after the sheep, taking them to places where there is plenty of grass to eat, leading them to the water so they can drink, and making sure they are safe from howling wolves and growling bears. A good shepherd loves his sheep and knows each of them by name, and he'll never leave them in danger, even if it means getting hurt himself.

Explain that Jesus talks about himself as being like our Good Shepherd. (Move the sheep around as you talk about God's care of us.) He looks after us and loves us, and knows each of us by name. (Mention each of the children and leaders' names.)

Praying

The Lord is my Shepherd,
(hold each finger in turn, so the ring finger is held on 'my')
there is nothing else I need.
(keep holding ring finger and shake head)

Activities

Today's prayer, from Psalm 23, can be learnt by heart, using the actions as a memory aid. Encourage the children to pray this whenever they feel frightened, holding on to their ring finger to remember that Jesus, the Good Shepherd, knows and loves them by name, and they belong to him. This teaching is reinforced on the sheet and the children can make a sheep, with their own name on it.

Notes

For parents to pray with your child

The Lord is my shepherd, there is nothing else I need.

Jesus knows us all by name

TIM

Write your name here.

Stick cotton wool on the sheep.

Stick the sides of the head together

FIFTH SUNDAY OF EASTER

Thought for the day

To produce fruit we need to be joined on to the true vine.

Readings

Acts 8:26-40; Psalm 22:25-31
1 John 4:7-21; John 15:1-8

Aim

To know they can be generous at passing on Jesus' love.

Starter

If you have access to a garden or patch of grass, give the children containers which you fill with water so they can go and water the plants. They can get a refill when their container is empty. Otherwise, play inside with water in washing-up bowls, funnels and containers.

Teaching

Talk about the way we were able to pour the water out on to the plants or into other pots because we had the water to use. What do we do at home if we need water to make a drink, or wash, or brush our teeth? We go and turn on the tap and out comes the water. If we get thirsty again, or need another bath after playing and being busy all day, we can go back to the tap and there's some more water waiting for us to use!

Have a bowl of water and a dry sponge. God's love goes on and on, and there's always plenty of it for us. Whenever we settle down with our friend Jesus (place the sponge in the water), we can't help soaking up some of his love, so we get more loving, just as this sponge is getting more wet by soaking up the water.

We can go back to soak ourselves in God's love every day, so that we are people filled with love. Then we can spread God's love around to other people and make the world a happy place.

Praying

Jesus, fill me up with your love
so I can spread love around
wherever it's needed!
Amen.

Activities

Each child will need an empty plastic pot. The children are going to decorate them with the picture and prayer which is on the sheet. There is also a picture to colour, of a gardener looking after a vine with grapes on it.

Notes

- Colour the prayer
- Cut it out
- Stick it round an empty pot
- Use your pot to spread water on plants!

For parents to pray with your child

Jesus, fill me up with your love so I can spread love around wherever it's needed! Amen.

How many bunches of grapes?

How many leaves?

How many butterflies?

Count and colour

SIXTH SUNDAY OF EASTER

Thought for the day

We are to love one another as Jesus loves us.

Readings

Acts 10:44-48
Psalm 98
1 John 5:1-6
John 15:9-17

Aim

To know that Jesus thinks of us as his friends.

Starter

Have an assortment of toys to play with, so that everyone can enjoy playing together as friends.

Teaching

Talk together about friends. Friends play together, giggle together and chat together. Friends stick up for one another and share things. Friends like being with each other. What do some of the children like about their friends? (Pass a soft toy around. This is held by the person who is talking, and the others listen.)

We are friends of Jesus. Jesus likes being with us and chatting with us, listening to our news and all the sad as well as the happy things. And he's always there for us – he doesn't suddenly go off us and not like us any more.

What do friends of Jesus do? They love one another, just as Jesus loves them.

Praying

Jesus, you are our friend and we are yours.
In all we think and speak and do
   (point to head, mouth and then open hands)
help us to love one another.
   (spread arms wide)
Amen.

Activities

On the sheet there are some pictures of people behaving like friends to tick, and some to cross out where people are not behaving lovingly at all. They can make a picture for Jesus to say 'thank you' for something in their life.

Notes

For my friend Jesus

Stick all kinds of things on to make a picture for Jesus or draw the people you want to thank God for.

Thank you, Jesus

Tick the pictures of people being friends

For parents to pray with your child

Jesus, you are our friend and we are yours.
In all we think and speak and do (point to head, mouth, then open hands) help us to love one another. (Spread arms wide)
Amen.

ASCENSION DAY

Thought for the day

Having bought back our freedom with the giving of his life, Jesus enters into the full glory to which he is entitled.

Readings

Acts 1:1-11 or Daniel 7:9-14
Psalm 47 or Psalm 93
Ephesians 1:15-23 or Acts 1:1-11
Luke 24:44-53

Activities

It is likely that Ascension Day services for schools will not need a separate programme for children. However, I have included a drawing and colouring activity for today so that children in church can work at this during the sermon.

SEVENTH SUNDAY OF EASTER

Thought for the day

Although now hidden from our sight, Jesus lives for ever, and in him we can live the Resurrection life even while we are on earth.

Readings

Acts 1:15-17, 21-26
Psalm 1
1 John 5:9-13
John 17:6-19

Aim

To hear about Jesus going back to heaven.

Starter

Hello, goodbye. As the music plays, the children skip and jump about. When it stops, they find another person, shake hands and say, 'Hello'. As the music starts again, they wave and say, 'Goodbye', before skipping and jumping off somewhere else.

Teaching

Our lives are full of hellos and goodbyes. Share some of the times we say hello and goodbye. Sometimes the goodbyes can be sad, if we've been with a special friend, or grandparents, and have to say goodbye to them. We know that means we won't be seeing them for a while.

Jesus' friends had got used to him being there to talk and laugh with. They loved being with Jesus. Even when Jesus had risen from the dead he would spend time with them sometimes. But now Jesus took his friends out to a hill and told them it was time to say goodbye. They wouldn't be seeing him any more as it was time for him to go back to heaven.

But Jesus wasn't going to leave his friends all alone. He loved them! He promised that in a few days he would send them a special present. When the present came they would be able to feel Jesus there with them all the time. That made the friends happy. They watched as a cloud took Jesus up out of their sight, and then they went back to Jerusalem to wait for the special present.

Praying

Be near me, Lord Jesus, I ask thee to stay
close by me for ever and love me, I pray.
Bless all the dear children in thy tender care,
and fit us for heaven to live with thee there.

Activities

The pictures of clouds and a crown can be coloured and hung together as a mobile. Or you can use the outlines as templates for white and gold thin card. The prayer can be stuck to one of the clouds.

Notes

For parents to pray with your child

Stick on cotton wool

Stick on cotton wool

Stick on cotton wool

JESUS

Be near me, Lord Jesus,
I ask thee to stay
close by me for ever
and love me, I pray.
Bless all the dear children
in thy tender care,
and fit us for heaven
to live with thee there.

PENTECOST

Thought for the day

The Holy Spirit of God is poured out in power on the expectant disciples, just as Jesus promised.

Readings

Acts 2:1-21 or Ezekiel 37:1-14
Psalm 104:24-34, 35b
Romans 8:22-27 or Acts 2:1-21
John 15:26-27; 16:4b-15

Aim

To celebrate the Church's birthday.

Starter

Pass the parcel. Beforehand prepare an outline picture based on the one below.

Cut flame shapes from coloured paper to fit exactly over the flames in the picture. Pack the flames into the layers of the parcel and the silhouettes of the disciples' heads in the 'prize' place. You can add a sweet if you wish! As each flame is unwrapped the child sticks it on to the right space, until the group has collectively completed the whole picture.

Teaching

Today we are celebrating! It's rather like the birthday of the Church, because today we remember how Jesus sent the Holy Spirit on his friends so they would be filled with God's love and power.

What did the Holy Spirit sound like? It sounded like a strong wind, blowing round the house. (All make the sound.)

What did the Holy Spirit look like? It looked like flames of fire. (Light twelve tea-light candles.)

What did the Holy Spirit feel like? It felt like being happy and excited and peaceful all at once, and wanting to tell everyone about how lovely it is to be loved by God.

Praying

Come, Holy Spirit,
and fill me up with God's love.
I may be small
and not very tall
but I can be BIG with God's love!
(Make yourself as big as possible)

Activities

The sheet can be made into a simple kite to fly. Each child will also need some cotton. Put reinforcers on the punched holes and staple the kites like this.

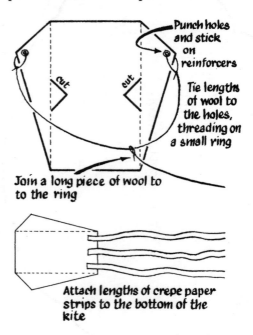

Punch holes and stick on reinforcers

Tie lengths of wool to the holes, threading on a small ring

Join a long piece of wool to to the ring

Attach lengths of crepe paper strips to the bottom of the kite

The kites should fly even in a very light breeze if the children run with them.

Notes

70

For parents to pray with your child

Come, Holy Spirit,
and fill me up with God's love.
I may be small
and not very tall
but I can be **BIG** with
God's love.

- Staple on lengths of flame-coloured crepe paper.
- Thread a small ring on a length of cotton and tie a long thread on to this.

CHECK FOR A SAFE PLACE TO FLY THE KITES

cut

cut

cut

cut

ORDINARY TIME

TRINITY SUNDAY

Thought for the day

The mysterious and holy nature of the one true God is beyond our understanding, but it is both communal harmony and individual personality, Father, Son and Holy Spirit.

Readings

Isaiah 6:1-8
Psalm 29
Romans 8:12-17
John 3:1-17

Aim

To learn about God from the wind.

Starter

Go outside and feel the wind. Work out where it's coming from, and watch what it does to such things as a piece of thread, a balloon, our clothes, and blown bubbles.

Teaching

Come back inside and sit in a circle, talking about the wind. What did it feel like on our skin? What did it do? Was the wind real? Could we see it? No! The wind and air are invisible, but we know they are very real. How? Because we can feel the wind and see what it does.

The wind is very useful because it can teach us about God. Like the wind, God's love and closeness to us can't be seen, but it is very, very real. We can feel that God loves us. We can see all around us the beautiful world God has made. Like the wind, we can see the good things God does.

Praying

I can't see the wind
but I can feel it's there.
I can't see you, Lord God,
but I can feel your love!

Activities

Using the sheet they can make a prayer wheel to hang in the wind, and there is a windy day picture for them to look at and colour, spotting the things the invisible wind is doing.

For parents to pray with your child

I can't see the wind
but I can feel it's there
I can't see you, Lord God,
but I can feel your love!

String goes through the straw. Hang the prayer wheel where the wind can blow it round.

GOD LOVES

Where's the wind? What's it doing?

Can you see the wind?

No, but I can see what the wind can do!

PROPER 4

Sunday between 29 May and 4 June inclusive
(if after Trinity Sunday)

Thought for the day

Jesus has the words of eternal life – he sheds light on a right attitude to the Law.

Readings

1 Samuel 3:1-10 (11-20) or Deuteronomy 5:12-15
Psalm 139:1-6, 13-18 or Psalm 81:1-10
2 Corinthians 4:5-12; Mark 2:23-3:6

Aim

To know that we are like clay pots holding God's treasure.

Starter

Have a number of boxes, pots and tins with a different thing in each. Name one of the objects and let the children guess which container it's in. Open each one to look until you find the right one. With the next object they may have seen it already, so memory as well as guesswork comes into the choosing. Continue till all the objects have been found inside their containers.

Teaching

Talk about how all those ordinary containers held different treasures. We've got some more containers here in Pebbles today. Count round the number of people present – we've got that number of treasure pots sitting here!

Each of us is like one of those ordinary pots, with secret treasure inside. The treasure is God's great love for us. (Gradually open up a huge red heart of paper.) Wherever we go and whatever we're doing, we know that God loves us, and that treasure makes us very special pots indeed! It means that we can be loving and kind, happy and strong because we haven't just got our loving in us – we've got God's as well.

Praying

I am filled with the love of Jesus –
love in my seeing,   love in my speaking,
   (point to eyes)   *(point to mouth)*
love in all I do.
   (open hands)
Thank you, Jesus,
   (raise arms)
your love is ENORMOUS!
   (stretch arms in huge circle)

Activities

Give each child a really big piece of paper cut into a heart shape. With paints or crayons they can make it very beautiful, as it is God's love they are drawing. Then help them to fold it up really small, so it will fit into the envelope made from the sheet, on which they draw themselves.

Notes

74

For parents to pray with your child

I am filled with the love of Jesus –
love in my seeing 👁
love in my speaking 👄
love in all I do.
Thank you, Jesus,
your love is ENORMOUS!

What treasure is in these pots? Draw it!

... and pop God's love inside

draw you on the envelope ...

GOD'S LOVE

PROPER 5

Sunday between 5 and 11 June inclusive
(if after Trinity Sunday)

Thought for the day

Anyone who does God's will is considered a close family member of Jesus.

Readings

1 Samuel 8:4-11 (12-15) 16-20 (11:14-15)
or Genesis 3:8-15
Psalm 138 or Psalm 130
2 Corinthians 4:13-5:1; Mark 3:20-35

Aim

To know that Jesus thinks of us as family when we do God's will.

Starter

Part of the family. Stand in a circle. Tell each group in turn the way to move in the circle, like this: 'If you are a brother, run in the circle; if you are a sister, skip round the circle; if you have an uncle, stand still in the circle; if you have a grandma, walk about in the circle.'

Teaching

Talk about the way we look a bit like other people in our family, and look for family likenesses in children from the same family, or with families everyone in the group knows well. Sometimes we are alike in the way we look and sometimes in how we walk, fiddle with our fingers, or laugh. Sometimes we are like other people in our family in being quiet or noisy, losing our temper or liking music.

One day Jesus was sitting talking to a circle of his friends, rather like we are sitting now. Someone told him that his mother, brothers and sisters were outside. Jesus looked around at all the people and told them he thought of everyone living God's way as part of his close family!

So that means us as well. We are part of Jesus' family, and when we are living God's way we're showing the family likeness.

Praying

(To the tune of *Twinkle, twinkle, little star*)

Jesus, Jesus, can I be
in your loving family?
When I live the loving way,
loving others every day,
Jesus, Jesus, I can be
in your loving family!

Activities

On the sheet there is a picture of Jesus sitting in a house surrounded by people who are listening to him. They add themselves to the group, and other people who are living as Jesus' friends. Also there is a praying space in which they can draw someone who doesn't know Jesus yet. As they draw this person meeting Jesus, they will be thinking of them and that is very real prayer.

Notes

You are all my family when you live God's way

Where are you?
Draw yourself listening
to Jesus

Think of
someone who
doesn't know Jesus
very well yet . . .

Draw them
meeting Jesus.
Pray for that
to happen

For parents to pray with your child

(To the tune of twinkle
twinkle little star)
Jesus, Jesus, can I be
in your loving family?
When I live the loving way,
loving others every day,
Jesus, Jesus, I can be
in your loving family!

PROPER 6

Sunday between 12 and 18 June inclusive
(if after Trinity Sunday)

Thought for the day

From small beginnings, and by God's power, the kingdom of heaven grows.

Readings

1 Samuel 15:34-16:13 or Ezekiel 17:22-24
Psalm 20 or Psalm 92:1-4, 12-15
2 Corinthians 5:6-10 (11-13) 14-17
Mark 4:26-34

Aim

To know that God's love grows and grows in his people.

Starter

Play with very soapy water, making bubbles by blowing through your hands. (Ordinary bubble mix is the rather boring substitute!) As you play, talk about the bubbles growing bigger and bigger, and see who can make the biggest.

Teaching

How did we make our bubbles grow? We had to blow very carefully and gently. Show the children some little seeds and pictures of what they grow into. Show them some real 'grown' examples as well if this is practical. In the story of Jack and the beanstalk, the beans grew up overnight into a huge plant, but usually the growing goes on bit by bit, day by day, until instead of a tiny seed you find a big tall plant, or even a tree.

Bubbles and plants aren't the only things which grow. *We* grow too! Let them stand up as tall as they can and remember when they were only very short. In the world God has made, there is lots and lots of growing that goes on.

Jesus told his friends one day that, just like the other things that grow, the kingdom of heaven grows and grows. Bit by bit God's love and goodness is growing and spreading. Once there were just a few of Jesus' followers, but now there are friends of Jesus all over the place. We know a few of them, because they are with us in our church. (Name some of them.) Then there are Jesus' friends in all the other churches, not just in this country, but all over the world.

Praying

Pray for each other by name:

Lord Jesus, bless . . . .
Let your love in her/him grow and grow
a bit more every day of her/his life.

Activities

When they have coloured and cut out the plant on the sheet, they can fold it as shown so that they can make it 'grow' like Jesus' love in us. They can also match the seed to the tree pictures.

Notes

Sycamore

Conker

Oak

Helicopter

Horse Chestnut

Acorn

Cut out

Fold

Fold

Fold

See the Flower grow!
... like us growing in God's love

Bubbles

Which bubble is the biggest?

Which bubble is the smallest?

For parents to pray with your child

Lord Jesus, bless _____
Let your love in her/him
grow and **grow**
a bit more every day
of her/his life.

Proper 7

Sunday between 19 and 25 June inclusive
(if after Trinity Sunday)

Thought for the day

What kind of person is this? Even the wind and waves obey him.

Readings

1 Samuel 17:(1a, 4-11, 19-23) 32-49 or
1 Samuel 17:57-18:5, 10-16 or Job 38:1-11
Psalm 9:9-20 or Psalm 133 or Psalm 107:1-3, 23-32
2 Corinthians 6:1-13; Mark 4:35-41

Aim

To know that Jesus calms our fears.

Starter

Bring either a small parachute or a large sheet and stand everyone around the outside, holding the edge. They can now make a flat calm, then build up through very gentle ripples to a full-blown storm, before making it die down again, ending with a gentle peace.

Teaching

Talk about what happens when we're frightened and about the people who calm us down and make us feel better. Also talk about any people and pets we calm down and comfort, when they're feeling frightened or worried.

Jesus is like that. When we are frightened or scared or upset, whether we're children or grown-ups, we can all come to Jesus and he will help to calm us down and comfort us. He may do that through your family, and he may use *your* words and arms to comfort other people or other creatures!

Sometimes you will find that as you ask Jesus to help you calm down, you will suddenly feel inside like our sheet was at the end of our pretend storm – all gentle and peaceful. Jesus is very good at bringing us peace, and all we have to do is ask for his help.

Praying

Give me your peace,
O Jesus Christ, my brother,
give me your peace,
O Jesus Christ, my Lord!

Activities

On the sheet there are pictures of a storm and a calm sea, children fighting and the same children playing together. Use these for spotting the differences, not just in the detail, but in what's going on. There is also space for them to draw in the calmed version of the pictured panic zone. Actively drawing the peace will help them work through the next conflict, Jesus' way.

Notes

For parents to pray with your child

Give me your peace,
O Jesus Christ, my brother,
give me your peace,
O Jesus Christ, my Lord.

Spot the difference

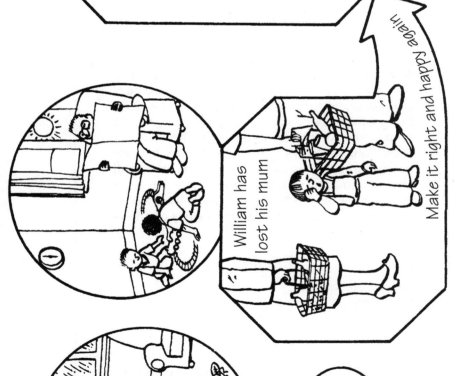

William has lost his mum

Make it right and happy again!

Spot the difference

Proper 8

Sunday between 26 June and 2 July inclusive

Thought for the day

God's power can reach even into death and draw out life.

Readings

2 Samuel 1:1, 17-27
or Wisdom of Solomon 1:13-15; 2:23-24
Psalm 130 or Psalm 30 or Lamentations 3:23-33
2 Corinthians 8:7-15; Mark 5:21-43

Aim

To know that Jesus is never too busy to bother with them.

Starter

Play the singing game *Here we go round the mulberry bush*, with lots of busy verses, such as 'This is the way we clean the car/carry the shopping/hoover the hall/make the packed lunches'.

Teaching

Talk together about being busy, and all the things that need to be done each day and each week. Sometimes we have to wait to tell our news or talk over a worry we have because people are too busy to listen straightaway. They might say, 'Just wait till I've got the dinner on', or 'till I've driven round this roundabout', or 'till we've paid at the checkout'.

But Jesus is always ready to listen to us, because he isn't stuck in time like us. He can give us his full attention straightaway, wherever we are. He never rushes us or tells us to wait. He's always ready to listen to our worries and fears, and enjoy our news and jokes with us.

Praying

Thank you, Jesus,
for listening when we pray.
You're never too busy to hear what we say.

Activities

There are pictures of some very busy animal life – ants, birds, bees and spiders – to talk about, with an observation activity. There is also someone telling some news, and they draw in a friend who is really listening to what she's saying. This discussion of what good listening involves will help the children become better at the skill themselves, as well as helping them understand that Jesus is the very best listener ever.

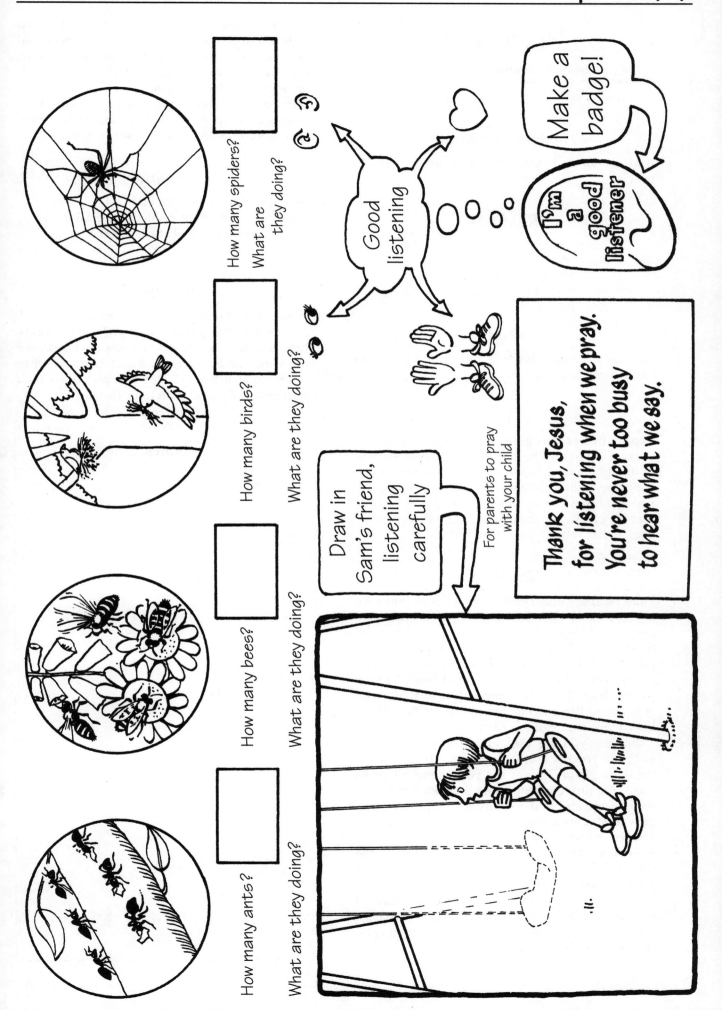

How many spiders?
What are they doing?

How many birds?
What are they doing?

How many bees?
What are they doing?

How many ants?
What are they doing?

Good listening

Make a badge!

I'm a good listener

Draw in Sam's friend, listening carefully

For parents to pray with your child

Thank you, Jesus, for listening when we pray. You're never too busy to hear what we say.

PROPER 9

Sunday between 3 and 9 July inclusive

Thought for the day

If we are not ready to listen to the truth, we will not hear it.

Readings

2 Samuel 5:1-5, 9-10 or Ezekiel 2:1-5
Psalm 48 or Psalm 123
2 Corinthians 12:2-10
Mark 6:1-13

Aim

To know that God talks to us and teaches us, and to learn about listening.

Starter

Explain that you are going to do a spot of listening today. Give out to the children pictures or models of different animals. Ask them all to shout to you the name of their animal or the noise it makes, and you will listen to what they are telling you. Finding that very hard, ask them instead to tell you one by one, so that you can hear them better.

Teaching

Point out how much easier it is to listen when we are quiet and still, without lots of other noises going on. One of the ways we pray to God is by making ourselves very quiet and still, so that we can listen to God's love, and feel him close to us.

Try being very quiet and still and listening for a pin to drop. Then try being still and quiet, with eyes closed (they can lie face down for this if they like), while you read this to them:

Imagine you are walking along beside a high wall and you see a little door in it. Over the door there is a picture of you and your name is written there. You turn the handle and the door opens. You walk inside and find a sunny day with soft green grass under your feet, and flowers growing there. You feel happy and safe in this place, and take off your shoes and run across the grass, enjoying the coloured flowers and the butterflies. You come to a sandy beach, and the sea is lapping against it, so you sit down and listen to the waves. Although you can't see him, you know that Jesus is here with you, and you sit quietly in the sunshine together by the sea, with the seagulls calling.

After a while you get up and walk back across the beach and the grass, put on your shoes and make your way to the door. As you go out of the door you know that you can come back to this garden of prayer whenever you like.

(Put on some very quiet music as you tell the children to sit up slowly and open their eyes. Pray today's prayer together while the music plays.)

Praying

O Jesus, we love to be with you!
Thank you so much for being our special friend, always here with us and always loving us.
Amen.

Activities

On the sheet there are lots of sounds 'pictured'. They look at the pictures and make the sounds. There is a checklist for top listeners – what do our eyes, ears, hands, brains, feet and heart do when we are really listening? They can also draw their own garden of prayer with Jesus there.

Notes

My garden of prayer

For parents to pray with your child

O Jesus, we love to be with you! Thank you so much for being our special friend - always here with us and always loving us.   Amen.

Top listener!

When we listen, we don't just use our ears

PURR!

STAMP!

What sounds are these?

POP!

CLAP!

QUACK! CHEEP!

BRMM!

PROPER 10

Sunday between 10 and 16 July inclusive

Thought for the day

Those who speak out God's will are bound to be vulnerable to rejection and abuse.

Readings

2 Samuel 6:1-5, 12b-19 or Amos 7:7-15
Psalm 24 or Psalm 85:8-13
Ephesians 1:3-14
Mark 6:14-29

Aim

To know that in Jesus they can stand up tall and upright for what is right in God's eyes.

Starter

Choose three different sounds (such as a bell, a shaker and a drum), and a grand, regal piece of music on tape such as *Land of hope and glory*. They move in a different way for each sound – such as crawling, jumping and bunny-hopping – but when the grand music plays they stand up tall and strong, like a good king or queen.

Teaching

Talk together about behaving well and being good (both adults and children), so that the children are telling you all they know about this. In voicing these good and noble things they will be reinforcing their own expectations of behaviour and beginning to own those values. Don't make any comments which contrast any of this with unacceptable behaviour, or the times we don't do it – we are simply celebrating the good we know about. Talk about how we behave well in different situations, such as in the car, at meal times, when playing with friends, when doing jobs at home. Help them to see that what they are describing is loving behaviour, thinking of other people and being kind and generous, honest and brave. It's Jesus behaviour, and it makes God very happy to see us doing it.

Praying

In your love, Lord Jesus,
I can stand up tall –
do what's right,
do what's good,
live the way I know I should.
In your love, Lord Jesus,
I can stand up tall!
Amen.

Activities

On the sheet there is a person to colour, cut out and fold so they stand happy and upright, living Jesus' way in the world. The whole sheet ends up being a landscape. Some of the children will need help with the cutting, and it's a good idea to have completed one sheet beforehand to show them what theirs will look like.

Notes

86

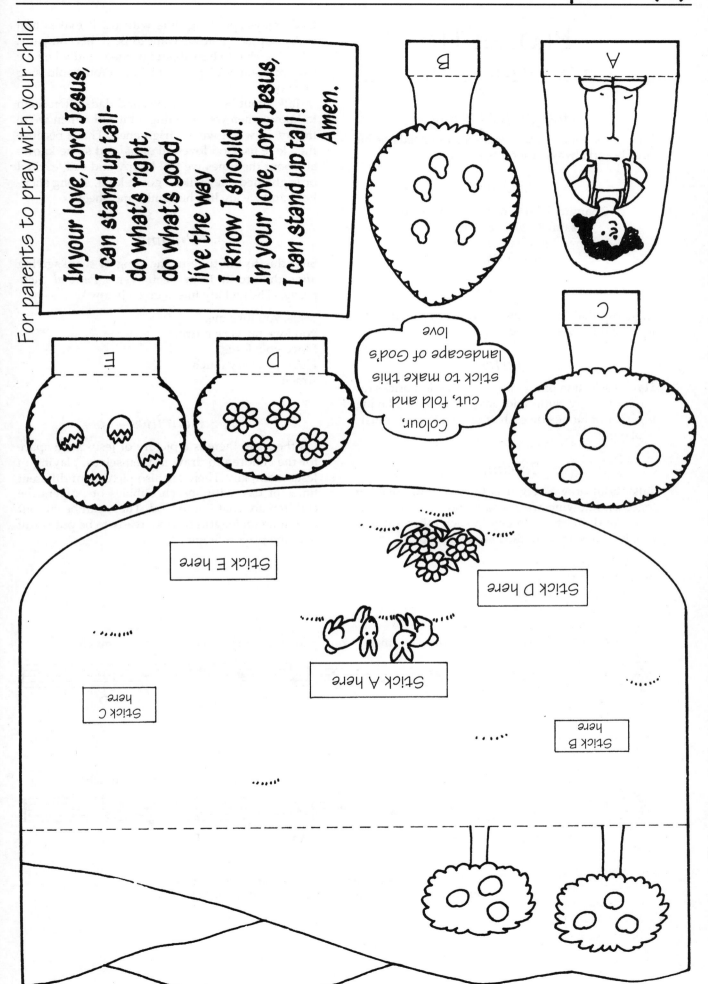

For parents to pray with your child

In your love, Lord Jesus,
I can stand up tall—
do what's right,
do what's good,
live the way
I know I should.
In your love, Lord Jesus,
I can stand up tall!
Amen.

Colour, cut, fold and stick to make this landscape of God's love

A
B
C
D
E

Stick E here
Stick D here
Stick A here
Stick C here
Stick B here

PROPER 11

Sunday between 17 and 23 July inclusive

Thought for the day

Like a good shepherd, Jesus sees the needs of his people and always responds with love.

Readings

2 Samuel 7:1-14a or Jeremiah 23:1-6
Psalm 89:20-37 or Psalm 23
Ephesians 2:11-22
Mark 6:30-34, 53-56

Aim

To know that Jesus likes them, enjoys their company and knows their needs.

Starter

Have a selection of toys and construction bricks (or boxes) to play with, and enjoy a time of playing together or alongside each other, while quiet music is playing.

Teaching

Talk about how lovely it is to enjoy time playing together, knowing we are safe and in God's good care. We didn't have to talk to each other – it was nice just to be there in the Pebbles group.

God enjoys spending time with us. It makes him really happy when we want to be in his company, when we chat to him about our ideas and when we sing our songs of praise to him. (You could sing one now.)

Talk about how our mums and dads often seem to know when we're feeling a bit sad, when we're thirsty, or when we are frightened. That's because they love us. God loves all of us, and so he knows all about the times we feel happy and sad, excited or frightened. He is like a good, kind, strong shepherd and we are like his lambs and sheep.

Praying

Sing this to the tune in the song of thanksgiving after the storm from Beethoven's *Pastoral Symphony*. (The melody line is given below.)

Jesus, you love me,
you love me very much;
I love you, Jesus,
I love you very much!
Amen.

Activities

On the sheet there is a picture of Jesus with space for the children to draw in themselves, playing in Jesus' company. There are also pictures of different times of day with speech bubbles of prayers the children are chatting to God. These can be cut out and hung on lengths of wool ready to be put up all over the place at home.

Theme from Beethoven's *Pastoral Symphony*, arr. Kate Gallaher
This arrangement © Copyright 1999 Kevin Mayhew Ltd

PROPER 12

Sunday between 24 and 30 July inclusive

Thought for the day

Out of God's riches, a great crowd is fed and satisfied from a small offering of food.

Readings

2 Samuel 11:1-15 or 2 Kings 4:42-44
Psalm 14 or Psalm 145:10-18
Ephesians 3:14-21
John 6:1-21

Aim

To know the story of the feeding of the crowd of people.

Starter

Prepare enough different coloured paper shapes for each child in the group to have one of each. There need to be as many different categories as there are children. Give each child a pile of a particular coloured shape so that everyone has a pile. (They can set up their own 'base', or have their shapes in a yoghurt pot.) All the children go round sharing the shapes out until they end up with a pile of different ones. These are arranged into a pattern on the floor in front of them.

Teaching

Admire everyone's patterns and talk about how we have all been sharing what we were given so that we could all make our lovely pictures. Today we are going to hear about a child who offered to share his lunch with Jesus.

Spread out a sheet or bath towel on the floor and sit around it. Place on it some blue material or paper to be a lake, and stand a few plants in pots around as bushes and trees. Place a model boat on the lake. Talk about the landscape you are making as you add the items, and let the children help.

One day Jesus and his friends went over the lake in a boat. All the crowds of people walked round the side of the lake (everyone finger walks), so they could be there when the boat arrived. Jesus climbed out of the boat and taught the people, telling them stories to help them understand how much God loved them.

Soon they were all very hungry, but they were a long way from their homes. One boy had some packed lunch with him. (Produce a packed lunch box.) He could have just sat and eaten it, but he knew the others were hungry too, and he heard Jesus talking to his friends about how to feed all these people.

So he went up to Andrew, one of Jesus' friends.

'Excuse me,' he said, 'but is this any use? There's five barley loaves and two small fish.'

Andrew took the boy and his lunch to Jesus, and Jesus looked very happy and thanked the boy very much for offering to share his food. 'Because you've been so kind, you've given enough here for everyone!' Jesus whispered to the boy. 'Watch carefully!'

Everyone sat down on the grass and Jesus gave thanks for the little lunch; he thanked God for providing enough for everyone, but the boy couldn't think how there would be enough. Jesus started breaking up the bread and the fish, and his friends kept taking it to the groups of people. Somehow the food went on and on, until everyone had eaten as much as they needed. And there was even some left over!

Praying

(This can be prayed before we eat.)

Thank you, God, for food we eat,
that keeps us strong and healthy.
Amen.

Activities

The Pebbles are going to make sandwiches, which can be cut up and shared with the rest of the congregation. If you want to be authentic you can have tuna or sardine sandwiches, but other fillings would be fine! On the sheet there is also a dot-to-dot picture of the boy's lunch, and a map for them to walk round with their fingers.

Notes

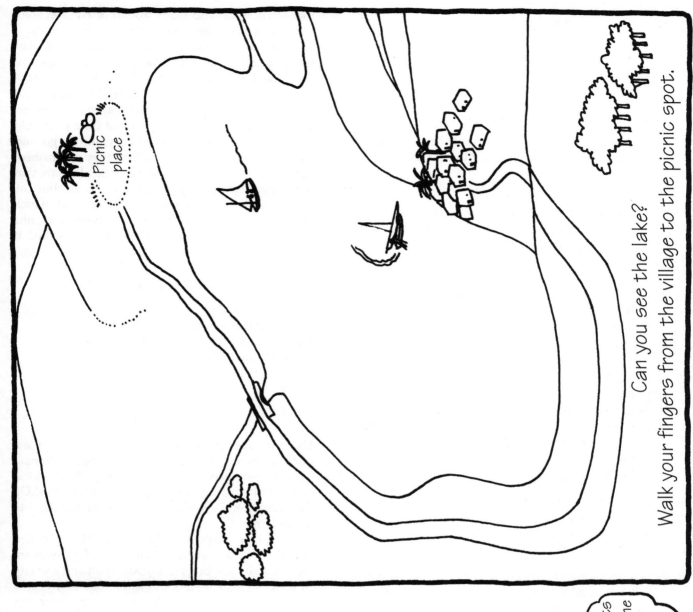

Can you see the lake?

Walk your fingers from the village to the picnic spot.

Picnic place

For parents to pray with your child

Thank you, God, for food we eat, that keeps us strong and healthy. Amen.

Join the dots to see what the boy had for lunch

PROPER 13

Sunday between 31 July and 6 August inclusive

Thought for the day

Jesus is the Bread of Life who satisfies our hunger and sustains us on our journey to heaven.

Readings

2 Samuel 11:26-12:13a or Exodus 16:2-4, 9-15
Psalm 51:1-12 or Psalm 78:23-29
Ephesians 4:1-16; John 6:24-35

Aim

To know that God gave the people of Israel food in the desert.

Starter

Manna? – What is it? Teach the children some Hebrew – that 'manna?' means 'what is it?' and then show them some items, mostly hidden in a bag or by a cloth. As you draw out a bit of a teddy, a jumper or an orange, you say to them, 'Manna?' so they can give the answer – 'It's a teddy!' Then a child can be the person who asks, 'Manna?'

Teaching

Remind the children, using a Moses basket, a crown, a whip of plaited string and a piece of blue cloth, that Moses was the baby who had been put in a basket and floated down the river to keep him safe when all God's people were slaves in Egypt. He was brought up by Pharaoh's daughter in the palace. When he grew up he had seen how his own people were badly treated as slaves. God used Moses to lead his people out of slavery. They had crossed through the middle of the Red Sea on dry land and now they were travelling in the desert, with Moses leading them.

And they got very hungry, so they all started grumbling. (Perhaps they start grumbling when they're hungry as well.) They said, 'It's not fair, Moses! If we were back in Egypt we could be eating nice stews and casseroles.' And they all got very grouchy with Moses.

Moses went off to talk with God about it. 'Lord, they're all moaning and grumbling about not having any food to eat,' he said. 'What should I do?'

God told Moses to let the people know that God knew they needed food and would be getting them some, so the people waited to see what would happen. That evening a flock of quails flew over. Some of the birds couldn't manage to fly any further, and they fell down dead on the ground. So the people picked them up and made a kind of chicken stew with them, and everybody enjoyed it very much.

Next morning there were white flakes all over the ground (scatter some pieces of white paper all over the floor). The people didn't know what it was, so they said to Moses, 'Manna? Manna?' And Moses said, 'This is the food God promised you!' So all the people took bowls (give out little pots) and gathered the white flakes. (The children go and gather it up in their bowls. When they've finished, they sit down again in the story circle.) Explain that our white flakes are just pieces of paper, but the flakes the people gathered up were food which tasted sweet – a bit like honey. And because no one knew what it was really called, they all called it 'manna'.

Praying

Thank you, God,
for giving us food each day.
Thank you for the farmers who grew it,
the shops that sell it,
and the people who cook it for us!
Amen.

Activities

Using a paper plate the children can make a plate of their favourite food out of playdough. Prepare some brown, green, yellow, red and white – most food can be made from roughly those colours! On the sheet there is a place mat to make for them to use at home.

Here is a recipe for playdough. Mix two teaspoons of cream of tartar, one cup of plain flour, half a cup of salt, one tablespoon of oil and one cup of water to form a smooth paste. Cook slowly in a saucepan until the dough comes away from the sides of the pan and forms a ball. When the dough is cool enough, take it out of the pan, add food colouring and knead for three or four minutes. (Store in an airtight container in the fridge.)

Notes

92

manna ?

THANK YOU, GOD!

Thank you, God,
for giving us food each day.
Thank you for the farmers
who grew it,
the shops that sell it,
and the people who
cook it for us!
Amen.

PROPER 14

Sunday between 7 and 13 August inclusive

Thought for the day

Just as bread is the visible form of life-giving nourishment, so Jesus is the visible form of God's life-giving love.

Readings

2 Samuel 18:5-9, 15, 31-33 or 1 Kings 19:4-8
Psalm 130 or Psalm 34:1-8
Ephesians 4:25-5:2
John 6:35, 41-51

Aim

To see God in the ordinary.

Starter

Share some ordinary things and look at them carefully. For example, bring a rosehip, break it open and look at all the seeds inside, a peapod with its neatly arranged peas, a selection of bright colours in feathers, flowers, stones and shells. Look up at the huge sky and the clouds, or the rain or shadows. Feel some wool, our hair. Work out how many sunrises there have been since they were born.

Teaching

Everything that we know and make, here in our exciting and beautiful universe, comes from something God has made. If we look carefully we can see God's love all around us in the things he has made. Look at all the objects again, helping the children to see how the great big sky over all of us is like the great big love God has for all of us. In the rosehip and the peapod we can see the loving way that God is careful with all the little things as well as the huge things. Each tiny seed and pea, each tiny baby, young child and little old woman is important to God.

God's love shines in our lives and warms our hearts, just as the sun shines on our bodies and warms us. The rain shows us how God showers us with blessings and happiness, without checking up first on how good we have been. And just as the sun rises day after day after day, so God is faithful and reliable, and we know we can trust him.

Praying

Your love is deeper than the sea
and wider than the sky.
You shower us with love
like you shower us with your rain –
lots and lots and lots of it!
The warm sun is just like
the warmth of your love.
And day after day after day
you forgive us
again and again and again!
Amen.

Activities

Provide some tubes for the children to look down, so they can focus on signs of God's love. They can also look through a magnifying glass at various things. On the sheet there is a magnified butterfly wing to colour in (or use collage), and they are encouraged to be observant, both physically and spiritually, in the 'What can you see?' activity.

Notes

For parents to pray with your child

Your love is deeper than the sea
and wider than the sky.
You shower us with love like you
shower us with rain-lots and lots
and lots of it! The warm sun is
just like the warmth of your love
and day after day after day
you forgive us again and again
and again!   Amen.

Look!

Look!

Look!

Some helping

Some loving and caring

Can you see God?

Look!

What can you see?

Something for packed lunch

No. But I can see
God in all the loving,
helping and giving!

PROPER 15

Thought for the day

God's wisdom may appear foolishness without the God-given grace to understand.

Readings

1 Kings 2:10-12; 3:3-14 or Proverbs 9:1-6
Psalm 111 or Psalm 34:9-14
Ephesians 5:15-20
John 6:51-58

Aim

To know that God helps us understand, and that he understands everything.

Starter

Have a time of sharing news, or let different children share with the others something they have learnt how to do.

Teaching

Spread all the pieces from a jigsaw puzzle over the floor in the circle, but don't show a picture of the completed puzzle. Talk about how we can put it together. First we can look for pieces with straight edges as they will make the edge of the picture. (Do this in turns.) Point out how much easier it would be if we had a picture to help us.

There are lots of things in life which are a big puzzle to us, and we find them very hard to understand. Perhaps we don't understand how dogs bark, why grown-ups talk so long on the phone, what makes heavy planes stay up in the sky, why Mum was cross with us that time, why Dad wasn't cross with us last week, how some people can be cruel to animals, why some people have asthma, why some people are very rich and others very poor.

Our life is full of puzzles. And we are always trying to work the puzzles out.

God understands all the puzzles, and knows why everything is as it is, and how. It's as if God holds the finished picture. So when we're puzzled about anything at all in life, we can ask God to help us understand. (Produce the jigsaw picture.) Bit by bit, if we keep working with God and with each other (talk as you work together on the puzzle), we'll start to understand some of those puzzles, even before we get to heaven!

Praying

Over the earth is a mat of green
over the green is dew,
over the dew are the arching trees,
over the trees, the blue.
Across the blue are scudding clouds,
over the clouds, the sun,
over it all is the love of God,
blessing us every one.

(Ruth Brown
© Oxford University Press)

Activities

The sheet can be made into a hanging model of today's prayer. Each child will need a circle of green paper stuck on thin card. The prayer is stuck on to this and the other layers made into circles as shown and fastened together with wool.

Notes

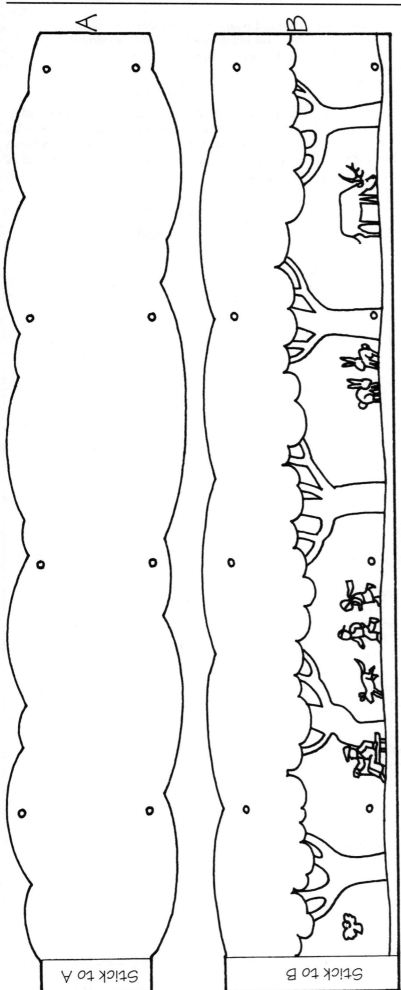

For parents to pray with your child

Over the earth
    is a mat of green,
over the green is dew,
over the dew
    are the arching trees,
over the trees, the blue.
Across the blue
    are scudding clouds,
over the clouds, the sun,
over it all
    is the love of God,
blessing us every one.

(Ruth Brown
© Oxford University Press)

GOD IS WISE

Q. What do you see when there is sun and rain together?

Q. What do rabbits live in?

Q. What colour is a robin?

green paper circle, 8 cm in diameter

PROPER 16

Sunday between 21 and 27 August inclusive

Thought for the day

'To whom else could we go? You alone have the words of eternal life.'

Readings

1 Kings 8:(1, 6, 10-11) 22-30, 41-43 or
Joshua 24:1-2a, 14-18
Psalm 84 or Psalm 34:15-22
Ephesians 6:10-20; John 6:56-69

Aim

To know that God gives us spiritual armour to protect us from evil.

Starter

Give the children lots of rolled-up balls of newspaper as snowballs and have either a leader or a child who volunteers to be the one everyone is trying to hit with the paper. However, this person is given a tray as a shield, to protect themselves.

Teaching

Talk about how much better it was to have the tray as a shield. It really helped to protect the person being pelted with snowballs! Have a look at some other things we use to protect ourselves – overalls and aprons protect our clothes from paint and glue, umbrellas and wet weather clothes protect us from getting too soaked, sunglasses protect our eyes from the glaring sun. If possible, have a look at some toy Roman armour, or a picture of a Roman soldier.

God knows that it isn't always easy to be loving and good, honest and kind. And he knows that sometimes people are hurt by bad things that happen, like wars, or someone being nasty to them, or frightening them, or making them feel silly. God hates to see any of his children getting hurt by any kind of evil, or hurting others. So he gives us armour to protect us from evil.

The armour is God's love, and if we imagine ourselves getting dressed in God's love every day, we'll be wearing his special armour to help us live God's way and fight against evil.

Praying

I am wearing the armour of God
to help me fight against evil.
I am carrying the shield of faith

'cos God wants me to be safe.
Yes, God wants me to be safe and strong,
and I belong to him!

Activities

On the sheet there is a picture of a Roman soldier and the children can dress him up in his armour by sticking on the cut-out sections. Talk with them about God's armour of love, goodness and faith as they work.

Notes

For parents to pray with your child

I am wearing
  the armour of God
to help me fight against evil.
I am carrying
  the shield of faith
'cos God wants me to be safe.
Yes, God wants me to be
  safe and strong,
and I belong to him!

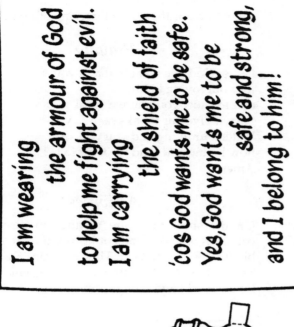

SHIELD

Proper 17

Thought for the day

We need to be careful never to replace the timeless commands of God with man-made traditions.

Readings

Song of Solomon 2:8-13 or Deuteronomy 4:1-2, 6-9
Psalm 45:1-2, 6-9 or Psalm 15
James 1:17-27
Mark 7:1-8, 14-15, 21-23

Aim

To look at how we can say 'thank you' to God with our lives as well as our voices.

Starter

Sit in a circle and pass round a paper plate or a broom stick. Each person mimes with the object to show what it is. (Examples might be a steering wheel or a fishing rod.)

Teaching

Point out how we managed to say what the plate or stick was, using not words but actions. In the circle try out some more telling actions, such as showing by our faces that we're pleased or grumpy, interested or scared.

Today we are going to look at some of the ways we can say 'thank you' to God for making us and such a lovely world, for forgiving us and looking after us.

We can say our thanks to God. Go round the circle with the children who want to thanking God for different things.

We can silently say our thanks to God. Suggest everyone shuts their eyes and puts their hands together, as we all thank God silently for something or someone special to us.

We can sing and shout and dance our thanks to God! Play and sing a favourite praise song, with the children singing along, dancing and playing instruments.

So we can tell God our thanks by saying aloud, saying silently, singing, shouting, dancing and playing . . . *and* by living our thanks.
How do we live our thanks?

Well, if we want to tell God how happy we are that he has made a lovely world, we can show him our thanks by being careful to look after it. (Chat together about ways this might be done.)

If we want to tell God how happy we are that he has given us loving people to look after us, we can show him our thanks by being helpful to those people. (Again, talk over examples.)

If we want to tell God how happy we are that he forgives us when we do things wrong, we can show him our thanks by forgiving other people.

Praying

Father God, we want to thank you
for your loving kindness,
and to show you that we thank you
we will live our thanks each day.
Watch our living and you will see
how loving and kind we'll try to be!
Amen.

Activities

On the sheet there are pictures to discuss and colour in of two friends of Jesus whose lives said a big 'thank you' to God. They are Saint Francis and Saint Clare, looking after the lepers, enjoying the lovely world and living simply.

Notes

Here is a friend of Jesus called **Clare**

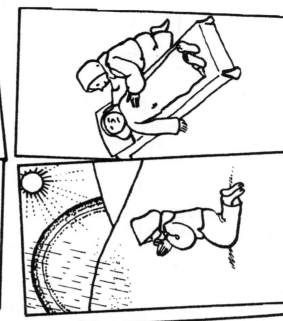

Here is another friend of Jesus, called

For parents to pray with your child

Father God, we want to thank you for your loving kindness, and to show you that we thank you we will live our thanks each day. Watch our living and you will see how loving and kind we'll try to be! Amen.

Here is a friend of Jesus called **Francis**

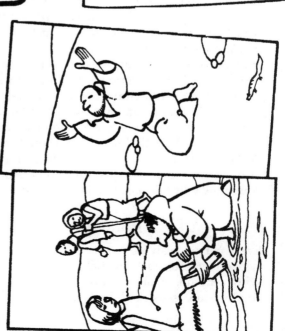

PROPER 18

Sunday between 4 and 10 September inclusive

Thought for the day

Jesus comes fulfilling the hope of healing to wholeness; he shows that mercy has triumphed over judgement.

Readings

Proverbs 22:1-2, 8-9, 22-23 or Isaiah 35:4-7a
Psalm 125 or Psalm 146
James 2:1-10 (11-13) 14-17; Mark 7:24-37

Aim

To know that God loves everyone whatever they look like and however rich or poor they are.

Starter

Have enough small gifts as prizes for each child to have one. Keep these hidden. Put some folded pieces of paper in a hat and tell the children that whoever picks the piece of paper with a smiley face on it will be able to have a prize! Hype this up a bit so they are all really hoping to be the lucky one. Pass round the hat, and tell each child to pick a piece of paper but not to open it until you say. When everyone has their paper, let them all open them up and discover that they have all won a prize. Give out the prizes with love from the church.

Teaching

Talk about what it feels like to be left out, and how it feels when we are the chosen ones. With our God no one is ever left out and we are all special to him, even though we are all different. God doesn't just love those with long hair in bunches, because God loves everyone! He doesn't just love those who are wearing stripes, because God loves everyone! Or those who eat without making a mess, because God loves everyone! He doesn't just love those who go to our church, or those on television. Why not? Because God loves everyone! He doesn't just love those who are good at football, or those who live with both Mum and Dad. Why not? Because God loves everyone! He doesn't just love nice people. He doesn't just love good people. Do you know why? *Because God loves everyone!*

Praying

Every person I can see
is loved by Jesus, just like me!
Whoever I am, whatever I do,
you love me, Jesus! And that's true.

Activities

On the sheet there is a picture of the earth with people all over it. The children can work out which ones Jesus loves by following a wiggly line with their finger. They can also make fingerprint pictures with their own special fingerprints that no one else has.

Notes

These fingerprints belong to

and nobody else in the world

Use your fingerprints to make some pictures which only you can make!

GOD LOVES EVERYONE!

God loves all the ones whose strings come here

Who does God love ?

PROPER 19

Thought for the day

Loving obedience to God is shown by Jesus to be a quality rich in courage and wisdom, a quality to be highly respected.

Readings

Proverbs 1:20-33 or Isaiah 50:4-9a
Psalm 19 or Wisdom of Solomon 7:26-8:1 or
Psalm 116:1-9
James 3:1-12
Mark 8:27-38

Aim

To look at how we can use our tongues to speak for good.

Starter

Tongue twisters. Try saying some of these: 'She sells sea shells on the sea shore'; 'red lorry, yellow lorry'; 'thirty thousand feathers on a thrush's throat'.

Teaching

Our tongues are very useful for talking. There are lots of sounds we can only make if we use our tongues – like ddd, ttt, nnn, ng, kkk, lll, sss. They can try making these sounds, noticing where their tongues go. Talking is a wonderful skill to have, and we start learning how to do it as soon as we are born. (Perhaps some of them have baby brothers and sisters who are just beginning to say the odd word.)

So now that we have learnt how to use our tongues for talking, what can we do with our talking? We can ask for exactly what we want or need, instead of crying and hoping someone will understand. We can tell other people what we are thinking. We can tell jokes. We can chat to our friends and we can pray to Jesus. We can cheer people up. We can help other people by telling them how to do something. (They can think of examples for all of these.) Put down a happy face and point out that we can use our tongues for saying all kinds of good and useful things.

Is that the only way we can use our tongues in talking? No, we could choose to use our tongues to say nasty, unkind things, or to be rude and disobedient, or to tell lies, or make someone cry. (Show an unhappy face.) But what a waste of a good tongue that would be. God has given us a wonderful gift of speaking. Let's use that gift to make the world a happier place.

Praying

Chatter, chatter, chatter,
thank you, God, for tongues to talk with,
tongues to tell the truth with,
tongues to speak kind words with,
tongues to pray and tongues to say,
chatter, chatter, chatter!

Activities

There are pictures on the sheet for the children to 'read' the sound effects, and also some situations with empty speech bubbles, where the children can work out what words could be said there.

Notes

104

PROPER 20

Sunday between 18 and 24 September inclusive

Thought for the day

The truly great in God's eyes are those who are prepared to be last of all and servant of all.

Readings

Proverbs 31:10-31 or Wisdom of Solomon 1:16-2:1,
12-22 or Jeremiah 11:18-20
Psalm 1 or Psalm 54
James 3:13-4:3, 7-8a
Mark 9:30-37

Aim

To know that God loves to see us looking after one another's needs.

Starter

Think of someone in the church community who would appreciate receiving a special 'get well soon' card from the Pebbles group (or whatever the need is). Explain this to the children and bring a suitable card along. Give each child a small piece of paper on which to draw a message, write the children's names on their drawings and stick them all into the card. The children can help put the card into its envelope and see it addressed and stamped.

Teaching

The Pebbles have done a very kind thing this morning, and that card will certainly cheer someone up. God loves to see us looking after one another's needs like that. It makes him very happy indeed!

Jesus always noticed what people were wanting, and went out of his way to help them. If he saw that someone was sad and lonely he would go and talk to them. When people came to him with their legs or backs not working, Jesus loved to mend their bodies and put them right. Jesus calls all his followers (and that's *us*!) to do the same thing – to look after one another's needs.

So how can we do that? What kind things could we do? Talk over their ideas and write them down. (It doesn't matter that they can't read them; they can see that you think they are important.) Read the list of suggestions back to them and give each of them a secret sign on their hand and your own (draw a smiley face) to remind you all of the kind things you and God are planning to do together. Suggest they do them as a secret between them and God.

Praying

Father God, we want to pray
for those who are sad or lonely,
for those who are ill,
for those who are very busy
and get tired from all their jobs.
Please help us to help them.
Amen.

Activities

The children can do another kind thing by making a scrap book of pictures and prayers to be passed around among those who would enjoy such a book. Provide a scrap book and some pictures for the children to cut out and stick in, and scribe for each child so that their prayers are also included. The pictures on the sheet can be coloured and added to the book.

Notes

For parents to pray with your child

Father God, we want to pray
for those who are sad or lonely,
for those who are ill,
for those who are very busy and
get tired from all their jobs.
Please help us to help them.
Amen.

PROPER 21

Thought for the day

Don't let your body lead you into sin and risk exchanging eternal life for eternal punishment.

Readings

Esther 7:1-6, 9-10; 9:20-22
or Numbers 11:4-6, 10-16, 24-29
Psalm 124 or Psalm 19:7-14
James 5:13-20; Mark 9:38-50

Aim

To know that it's good to pray for one another.

Starter

Prepare a prayer area which looks beautiful and special, with lights and flowers, pictures and a cross. It might include a mirror lying flat so that everything is reflected. Have quiet music playing and gather the children to sit round, to sing a quiet worship song such as *Jesus, reign in me* or *Jesus, I adore you*. Then all pray for each of the children in turn by name, like this:

Jesus, we ask you to bless Sean
with your love in his life.
We thank you for his funny jokes
and the way he cheers us up.
We ask you to help him and his family
as they get ready to move house soon.
Be with Sean every day of his life.
Amen.

The other children can stretch one hand up to God and the other towards the child being prayed for to remind them 'in body' that they are being channels of God's love as they pray.

Teaching

It's good to pray for one another. It's good to know that other Christians are praying for us. Praying is the way that God helps us look after one another and deepen our love for one another. Today we're going to learn a bit more about how to pray.

Show the children a walking stick, zimmer frame or crutches, and talk with them about who uses these and why. Imagine together what it must be like just to need help walking, and to be in pain, let alone losing the use of your legs. When we pray for people, we need to imagine what it's like for them, and feel sorry for them. Then we ask our lovely Jesus to help those people. (Do this.) Jesus has lots of ways of helping someone. Sometimes he helps by making their legs strong again so they work. Sometimes he makes the person happy and peaceful even though their legs still don't work. Whatever is best and right, Jesus will do when we pray, trusting him.

Show the children a watering can, with water inside. When we pray, Jesus can pour out his love through us so that it reaches other people who don't pray. (Pour out the water so it sprinkles over a plant.) When we pray we are like channels of God's love. We reach up to God (reach up one hand), letting him fill us with his love, and send it out over the places and people in the world who need it (stretch out other hand). As they are in this position ask them to close their eyes and think of God's love coming into them and them pouring that love over the people who are sad at the moment, all over the world. 'Jesus, fill us now with your love. Let that love pour out over all the people who are sad, so that they feel your love and peace instead of their sadness. Amen.'

You can tell them that children are specially good at praying because they are so good at trusting God. God enjoys working with children of their age – they don't have to wait until they're older.

Now they can practise, talking about people they feel need praying for, and all the children praying together in their own words, for this person or situation. Thank God for answering all our prayers and letting us work with him to spread his love and peace.

Praying

Jesus, show me
who to pray for
and what to pray for.
Thank you for having me
on your prayer team. Amen.

Activities

The sheet can be made into a prayer corner for their bedroom. They will need thin card to strengthen it and a hole punch and some cord or wool to fasten it.

Notes

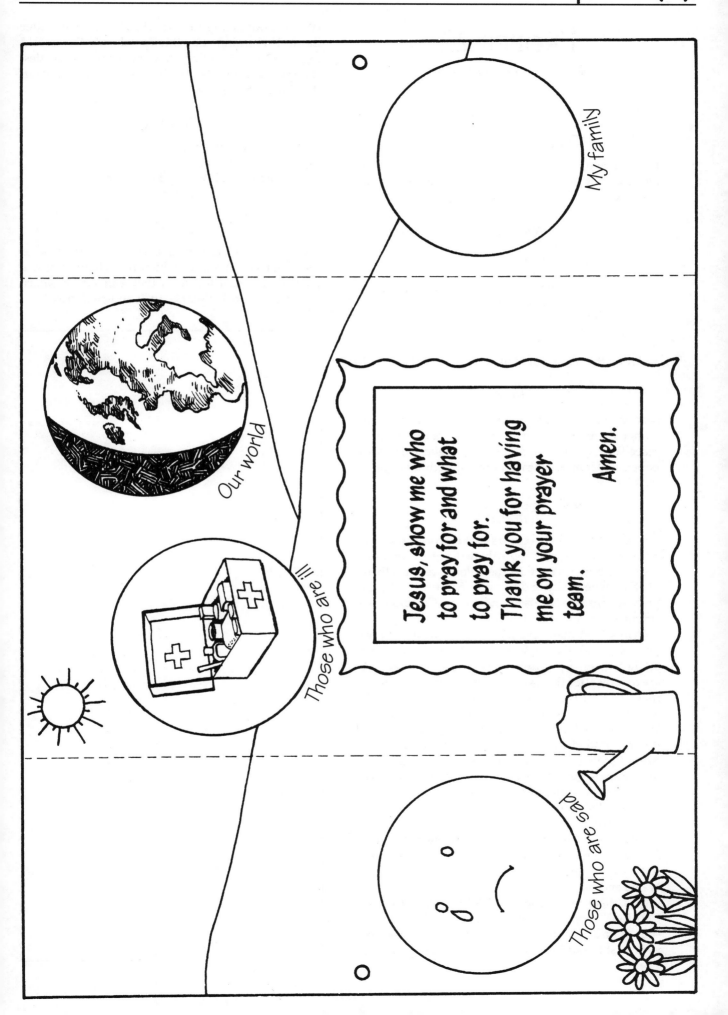

My family

Our world

Those who are ill

Those who are sad

Jesus, show me who to pray for and what to pray for.
Thank you for having me on your prayer team.

Amen.

PROPER 22

Sunday between 2 and 8 October inclusive

Thought for the day

Human beings are made responsible for the care of creation but are subject to God in all aspects of their lives.

Readings

Job 1:1; 2:1-10 or Genesis 2:18-24
Psalm 26 or Psalm 8
Hebrews 1:1-4; 2:5-12
Mark 10:2-16

Aim

To know that God wants us to look after the world.

Starter

Scatter around some fallen leaves. The children gather them up one at a time and bring them to place them on brown, red, orange, yellow or green paper, matching the leaf to the approximate colour of the paper.

Teaching

Talk about the lovely colours of our world in all the different seasons, and show them different coloured pieces of paper. What do the colours remind them of? (The blue of sky and sea and forget-me-nots, the pink of sunsets and roses, and so on.) Celebrate the colourful world God has made.

When God made people, he gave us an important job to do. We are to look after this world, and all the universe, as carefully as we possibly can. We are to look after the ground (place down a chunk of rock) and all the minerals of our planet like gold and silver, iron and copper, calcium and sulphur. We are to look after all the growing plants (place down a potted plant) like rain forests and cactus, fruits, flowers and herbs. We are to look after all the animals (place down a book of animals and turn through some of the pages) like horses, fish, birds, spiders and worms.

And we are to look after one another (place down a book with pictures of people from all different parts of the world and flick through it), sharing so that everyone has enough to eat, and taking care of one another.

Are there any Pebbles who are ready to help God look after the world? That's good! Could we start today? How? Talk over their ideas and do your best to put into practice any that are practical.

(What about giving each child a bag to collect litter in and cleaning up this patch of the world together? Or recycling their newspapers, bottles, stamps and cans?) Scribe the ideas and put them in the church magazine.

Praying

Father God, we love this world
that you have made.
We are old enough to help look after it
and we're going to start by . . .

Activities

Use the leaves from the starter activity to stick on the sheet and make leaf pictures. There is also a picture of a rain forest so they can go on safari, hunting for hidden plants, fruit and creatures.

Notes

This is my picture made of leaves

What can you see in the rain forest?

For parents to pray with your child

Father God, we love this world that you have made. We are old enough to help look after it and we're going to start by

. . . .

PROPER 23

Thought for the day

The word of God is living and active, piercing right to the heart; only with God is it possible to be saved.

Readings

Job 23:1-9, 16-17 or Amos 5:6-7, 10-15
Psalm 22:1-15 or Psalm 90:12-17
Hebrews 4:12-16
Mark 10:17-31

Aim

To know that we are to seek God and find him, and help others to do the same.

Starter

Set up an edible treasure hunt, leading the children from one numbered box to the next. Spread the boxes around the edges of the room. Give them each a length of string, with a twiglet tied to one end. (This stops them losing the other things off the end.) In numerical order they thread on an object from each box. They should each end up with their strings looking identically threaded. Box one contains hula hoops (the edible sort) box two has polos, box three has jelly rings and box four has biscuits with a hole in the middle. Those with the right order on the string can eat their necklace.

Teaching

Talk about our funny treasure hunt. We had to seek for the right number on the box, and get that right. Then we had to do something with what we found. That led us on to the next thing to seek – we found the treasure as we went along, didn't we? And it was treasure that tasted good.

The Bible tells us that we are to seek God as we live our lives. It's a bit like our treasure hunt. We seek, or search, for God by looking out for his love, just as we looked out for the numbers on the boxes. We might find God's love in helping someone, being friendly, enjoying God's beautiful world or talking over our fears and worries with God. There are lots of different ways we can find God's love around, just as there were lots of different tasty things to thread on our string. Our strings were filled up with all sorts of tasty things, and our lives will be filled up with the love of God as we seek him.

Seeking God will help us to know what is right and good, and that will make us happy as Jesus' friends.

Ask if any of them helped someone to find any of the boxes. Thank them for doing that. God wants us to help others to seek him as well. We could invite them to Living Stones, or lend them one of our favourite Bible stories, and we can pray for them. That way we will be helping them to get to know our lovely God.

Praying

As I get to know you, Jesus,
I love you more and more.
You're kind and good,
you're strong and brave,
and I'm glad you are my friend.

Activities

On the sheet there are pictures of children who are seeking God in different ways, and they can circle the ones they do as well, or want to start doing. There is space for them to draw a person they want to help to seek God.

Notes

112

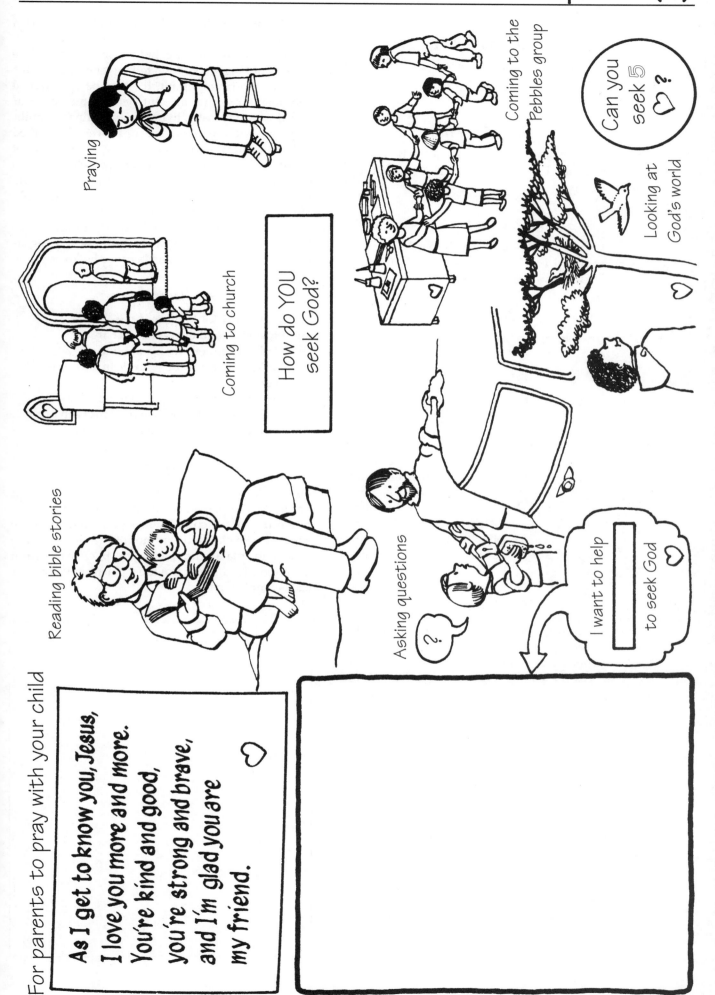

Praying

Coming to the Pebbles group

Can you seek 5 ♡ ?

Looking at God's world

Coming to church

How do YOU seek God?

Reading bible stories

Asking questions

I want to help _____ to seek God ♡

For parents to pray with your child

As I get to know you, Jesus,
I love you more and more.
You're kind and good,
you're strong and brave,
and I'm glad you are
my friend. ♡

PROPER 24

Sunday between 16 and 22 October inclusive

Thought for the day

Even the Son of Man himself came not to be served but to serve, and to give his life as a ransom for many.

Readings

Job 38:1-7 (34-41) or Isaiah 53:4-12
Psalm 104:1-9, 24, 35c or Psalm 91:9-16
Hebrews 5:1-10; Mark 10:35-45

Aim

To know that Jesus is a Servant King.

Starter

Yes, your majesty. You will need a small handbell. One child is the king (or queen) and wears a crown. The others are all the king's servants, and they do all the work at the palace. Whenever the king rings his bell, the servants have to run up to where he is and bow or curtsey. Then the king gives his command (with the leader's help) and the servants rush about doing what he says. A leader takes the king to different parts of the palace for ringing the bell. Commands are household jobs, such as 'Sweep the floor!', 'Make the bed!', 'Clean the windows!' and 'Peel the potatoes!'

Teaching

Put down the crown, and a dustpan and brush. Hold the appropriate symbol as you refer to kings and servants. What is a king? A king is the person who rules over a land and is in charge of it. (We're thinking about traditional, storybook kings here, as this is in keeping with the imagery Jesus uses.) He's the one who gives the orders and tells everyone else what to do. He knows he is powerful and expects everyone to bow or curtsey to him, and say, 'Yes, your majesty!' to him. (The children can try that out, with another child wearing the crown and strutting about importantly.)

What is a servant? They are the ones who do the work, looking after the king and his family, and making sure he has all the things he needs. The servants cook and clean, and do the washing, and tidy up, and buy the food, and weed the garden, and clean out the gerbils, and put out the rubbish, and polish the tables, and scrape mud off the shoes . . . ! (The children can try all these out in quick succession, till everyone is out of breath.)

Who would they rather be – the king or a servant?

Now Jesus is our King, but he isn't anything like the sort of king we've been talking about, is he? It's true he is very important. It's true he is powerful and reigns over us all. But Jesus came into our world as a tiny baby, living in an ordinary family, like ours, without any palace or power. He worked as an ordinary carpenter, making things out of wood. In fact, Jesus is a king, but he behaves like a servant! He went around looking after people, making them better and cheering them up. He looks after us now, helping us wherever we need help.

(Put the crown over the dustpan and brush.) So Jesus is both a king *and* a servant, not bossing us around but caring for us all because he loves us.

Praying

Leader: We pray for kings and queens
and presidents and everyone in charge.
All: Lord, make them wise and good.
Leader: We pray for those who clean and cook
and everyone not in charge.
All: Lord, make them wise and good.
Leader: Our Servant King, we pray for each other.
All: Lord, make us wise and good. Amen.

Activities

On the sheet is a game to play with the king giving orders to the players who are the servants. They mime the jobs pictured when they land on those squares. The children can mount the sheet on thin card and make the pieces to play with from coloured playdough. Provide a plastic envelope for each complete game.

> ## Notes

For parents to pray with your child

Parent We pray for kings and queens and presidents and everyone in charge.

Both Lord, make them wise and good.

Parent We pray for those who clean and cook and everyone not in charge.

Both Lord, make them wise and good.

Parent Our Servant King, we pray for each other.

Both Lord make us wise and good. Amen.

- Thow the dice
- Look at the picture
- Mime the action

wash the dishes

brush the cat

walk the dog

put the kettle on

hang out washing

sweep the floor

weed the garden

paint the door

clean the car

clean my shoes

mow the grass

polish my crown

count the sheep

make the bed

PROPER 25

Thought for the day

In Jesus, God gathers his scattered people and opens their eyes to see.

Readings

Job 42:1-6, 10-17 or Jeremiah 31:7-9
Psalm 34:1-8, 19-22 or Psalm 126
Hebrews 7:23-28
Mark 10:46-52

Aim

To know that Jesus helped a blind man to see.

Starter

I spy with my little eye . . . using either colours, or letter sounds.

Teaching

Tell the story of Bartimaeus while you (or an assistant!) draw it on a black or white board, rubbing out and changing things as you go. Very simple drawings are fine, and most effective. The visuals are there to aid imagination, not replace it. Basically you'll be drawing Bartimaeus begging by the road, a crowd of people coming in a cloud of dust down the road, the disciples' cross faces, the disciples turning friendly, Bartimaeus meeting Jesus, and Bartimaeus happy and able to see.

Praying

With my eyes, Lord, I can see
all the love you have for me.
Help me spread your love to others,
friends and parents, sisters, brothers,
till the world is full of love.

Activities

On the sheet the children can make a face with closed eyes which open. There are also hidden things for them to use their eyes to find in the picture.

Notes

A

Cut out

Cut out

A

For parents to pray with your child

With my eyes, Lord, I can see
all the love you have for me.
Help me spread your love to others,
friends and parents, sisters, brothers,
till the world is full of love.

Can
you
see

ALL SAINTS' DAY

Sunday between 30 October and 5 November inclusive

Thought for the day

Great is the rejoicing in heaven among the saints of God as they worship their Lord in glory.

Readings

Wisdom 3:1-9 or Isàiah 25:6-9
Psalm 24:1-6
Revelation 21:1-6a
John 11:32-44

Aim

To know that Jesus' friends get to party in heaven.

Starter

Party games. Give everyone a party hat and play a couple of party games such as animal statues. (You tell them which animal to be and when the music stops they freeze in this species. Then they become a new animal.)

Teaching

We're having quite a party today because we're joining in with all the saints in heaven.

When close friends of Jesus die, that isn't the end of their life. They are welcomed into heaven by Jesus and all the angels, who are very happy to see them. They may have come into heaven tired and worn out from doing lots of good and loving things on earth all through their life, but now all their tiredness goes away and they feel like dancing and singing! They might have known sadness on earth, but when they get to heaven, all their tears are wiped away, and they are filled with happiness and joy instead.

They are really happy to meet their friend Jesus face to face, and it's wonderful to be in all the light and beauty of heaven, where there is nothing nasty or evil, nothing selfish or unkind, but only all that is good and lovely.

All close friends of Jesus will get that welcome in heaven when they die. And the happiness is not just for an afternoon or a week. It lasts for ever and ever and ever!

Praying

Bless all the dear children
in your tender care,
and fit us for heaven
to live with you there.

Activities

Continue the party with a few nibbles, and some singing and dancing, praising God. On the sheet there are instructions for making a musical instrument. Each child will need a plastic bottle, some dried peas and some lengths of crepe paper.

Notes

For parents to pray with your child

Bless all the dear children in your tender care, and fit us for heaven to live with you there.

DRIED PEAS

Crepe paper

Bottle

1 2 3 4

Well done

Stick the food on the table

Fourth Sunday before Advent

Sunday between 30 October and 5 November inclusive*

* For use if the Feast of All Saints was celebrated on 1 November and alternative propers are needed

Thought for the day

To love the living God with heart, soul and strength, and to love our neighbour as ourselves means far more than any sacrificial offerings.

Readings

Deuteronomy 6:1-9
Psalm 119:1-8
Hebrews 9:11-14
Mark 12:28-34

Aim

To learn the summary of the law.

Starter

Have lots of building bricks or cartons for the children to play with, balancing one on another to construct towers and buildings.

Teaching

We were building on the good strong floor, and that helped us build good strong towers. The Bible tells us two good strong rules to build our lives on, and we're going to learn them off by heart, so that we'll always have them inside our minds, and won't lose them or drop them.

The first and most important is to love God (point up), with all our hearts (hands on heart), with all our mind (hands hold head), and with all our strength (flex arm muscles). And the second is to love other people as we love ourselves.

Teach the children to sing this summary of the law to the tune of *London's burning*. The accompanying actions will help them to learn the words and understand them.

You shall love the
(hands on heart)

Lord your God with
(point upwards)

all your heart and
(hands on heart)

all your mind and
(hold head with hands)

all your strength! All your strength!
(show biceps)

And love each other, and love each other.
(arms round one another's shoulders)

Read verse 7 in Deuteronomy 6 to them, explaining that grown-ups have been passing on this rule to their children and grandchildren and great-grandchildren for thousands of years, and now you are passing it on to them. When they grow up and have children they are to pass it on to their children and their grandchildren to make sure that everybody knows it really well, and can live by God's love every day.

Praying

I love you, Lord God,
with all my heart and mind and strength!
Amen.

Activities

The children can decorate the summary of the law with stickers, printing or stencils. It can then be tied on to a chair or door at home to remind them of God's rule of love.

Notes

THIRD SUNDAY BEFORE ADVENT

Sunday between 6 and 12 November inclusive

Thought for the day

When we are called we need to respond with obedience so that many may be brought to repentance.

Readings

Jonah 3:1-5, 10
Psalm 62:5-12
Hebrews 9:24-28
Mark 1:14-20

Aim

To know that Jesus called the fishermen to follow him.

Starter

Play the fishing game, using either a commercial version or a homemade one – coloured paper fish with paperclips, and pea-stick fishing rods with string lines and opened paperclip hooks. Use a (dry) paddling pool, scatter the fish in it and stand each rod in a wellie. The children can hook the fish and throw them back in.

Teaching

Jesus lived beside a big lake which had lots of fish in it. That meant there were fishing boats, and fishermen who went and caught fish to sell. Invite the children to be fishermen, and do all the actions of mending the nets so there aren't any big holes, and scrubbing the boat out to keep it clean. Then they have to push the boat off from the shore, wade out and climb in the boat, hoist the sail and steer the boat. They let down the anchor, throw the fishing nets out into the water and wait. Then when the net is full of fish they haul the heavy net in, tip the fish into baskets at the bottom of the boat and sail back to the shore. They jump out of the boat and haul it up the beach. Then they have to carry the baskets full of fish to sell in the market. After all that they can lie down and have a bit of a rest while they listen to a story!

One morning a man called Jesus was walking along the beach. He was looking for some people to help him in his work, and he saw the fishermen. Some of them were throwing their nets into the water. (And we know how to do that, don't we?) Some of them were sitting on the beach mending their nets. (And we know how to do that, don't we?)

And Jesus thought fishermen, who are good at catching fish, would be just the people he needed to reach people for God. Fishermen who mended their nets would be just the people he needed to mend people through God's love. So he called them to follow him. 'Follow me!' he said.

And the fishermen were happy to follow Jesus and work with him.

Praying

If I was a fisherman
  (mime fishing)

and Jesus called me,
  (cup hand to ear)

I'd throw down my fishing nets
  (do that)

and run to his side.
  (run on the spot)

I am a child and Jesus calls me.
  (point to yourself, and cup hand to ear)

I say, 'Here I am!'
  (shout it, waving at the same time)

and run to his side.
  (run on the spot)

Activities

Each child will need a piece of old net fabric, about the size of a handkerchief. There are fish to colour and cut out on the sheet and these can be put in the net which is then tied up with a rubber band or length of string or wool.

Notes

For parents to pray with your child

If I was a fisherman   (mime fishing)
and Jesus called me,   (cup hand to ear)
I'd throw down my fishing nets   (do that)
and run to his side.   (run on spot)
I am a child   (point to self)
and Jesus calls me.   (cup hand to ear)
I say, 'Here I am!'   (shout it, waving)
and run to his side.   (run on spot)

SECOND SUNDAY BEFORE ADVENT

Sunday between 13 and 19 November inclusive

Thought for the day

We are to be on our guard; great anguish will accompany the last days, but all that is good and loving, wise and true will be saved and celebrated for ever.

Readings

Daniel 12:1-3
Psalm 16
Hebrews 10:11-14 (15-18) 19-25
Mark 13:1-8

Aim

To know that love lasts for ever and heaven is full of it.

Starter

Give out chocolate buttons to suck and see who can make theirs last the longest.

Teaching

Some things only last as long as a chocolate button. They are nice to suck but we know they won't last for ever. Bubbles don't last long either. (Blow a few and enjoy their colours and roundness, until they pop.) Lots of good things are with us for just a little while, so it's a good idea to really enjoy them while we have them.

Some things, like long journeys, or grown-up conversations, seem to go on for ages and ages! But they don't go on for ever. In the end, it's time to get out of the car, or the grown-ups say goodbye and we can carry on walking to the swings.

What will last for ever and ever and ever? To give them a clue, show them a red heart shape. It's *love* that will last for ever, and that's because our God is Love, and God lasts for ever and ever. What kind of loving things do we do? (Share ideas.)

One day, at the end of everything, God will gather up all that goodness and love into his heaven, so it's safe for ever, and not one bit of it will be lost.

Praying

God of love, we thank you
for all the love in our world.
What a good thing that love
lasts for ever and never wears out!

Activities

On the sheet there is the shape of a heart. The children cover this with glue and then sprinkle glitter, sand or tiny off-cuts of shiny paper on to the page. At the moment they can't see what will stay and what won't, but when they shake their sheet, the thing that lasts is the love.

Notes

CHRIST THE KING

Sunday between 20 and 26 November inclusive

Thought for the day

Jesus Christ is the everlasting King whose kingdom is not of this world, but grows in the hearts of his people and lasts for ever.

Readings

Daniel 7:9-10, 13-14
Psalm 93
Revelation 1:4b-8
John 18:33-37

Aim

To celebrate Jesus as our King.

Starter

Everyone helps decorate the room with paper chains and gold crowns. Then sing and dance to some praise songs, using recorded music such as the *Kid's Praise* albums.

Teaching

Talk about the dreams we have, and then tell the children the vision of Daniel as a story, like this.

Long, long ago there lived a man called Daniel. Daniel worshipped God and tried his best to live God's way. In the days of King Belshazzar, king of Babylon, Daniel had a dream. It was such an amazing dream that he couldn't get it out of his head. Daniel kept thinking about his dream, and in the end he realised that the dream had been given to him by God. So Daniel thought to himself, 'If God has shown me these amazing things in my dream, I expect he wants me to tell all the others about it.'

So Daniel wrote his dream down, and this is it.

'As I looked, I saw a great throne put in its place, and God Almighty sat down on the throne. His clothes were as shining white as snow. His hair was white like sheep's wool. His throne was flaming with fire, blazing and glowing. From the throne there ran a river of fire, pouring out, and burning brightly. Thousands and thousands of people were standing before the throne, as if they were waiting for something. The books were opened.

'Then I saw in front of me what looked like a man. He was coming with the clouds of heaven, closer and closer to Almighty God, and they led him up to the throne. This man was made King over all the people in every place and every time. And as I looked I knew that he would be King for ever and ever and ever.'

That was the dream which Daniel dreamed long, long ago. Long before Jesus had been born. And yet God had shown Daniel a picture of heaven, and he had seen Jesus, coming into heaven and being made King for ever.

Praying

Jesus, you are my King.
Reign in me and my home,
reign in my life for ever.
Amen.

Activities

Together make a large collage picture of Daniel's dream. Have the outline drawn already (based on the picture below) and bring some shiny flames of fire for the children to stick on to the throne and the fiery river. They can stick wool on to the clouds and coloured tissue paper to the rest of the picture. Call the picture: Daniel's dream about heaven.

On the sheet the same picture is there for them to colour or build with collage, and they can find the matching crowns and flames.

Notes

For parents to pray with your child

Jesus, you are my King.
Reign in me and my home.
reign in my life for ever.
Amen.

Colour this picture of Daniel's dream

Can you match up the flames?

Can you match up the crowns?

Prayer for Second Sunday before Lent

All that we can hear and ev-ry-thing we can see, in-clud-ing

C   F(Dm)   Am   F(Dm)

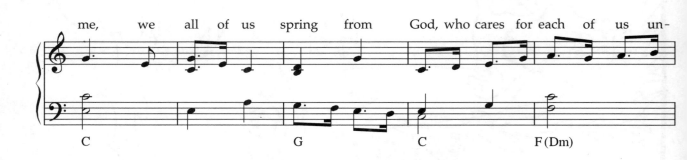

me, we all of us spring from God, who cares for each of us un-

C   G   C   F(Dm)

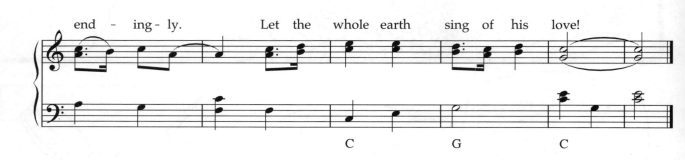

end - ing - ly. Let the whole earth sing of his love!

C   G   C

Words: Susan Sayers
Music: Susan Sayers, arr. Noel Rawsthorne
© Copyright 1986 Kevin Mayhew Ltd